THE LONGCHEN NYINGTHIG CHOD PRACTICE "SOUND OF DAKINI LAUGHTER"

LITURGY BY JIGMEY LINGPA, PROFOUND INSTRUCTIONS BY PATRUL, AND COMMENTARY BY THE AUTHOR

BY TONY DUFF

PADMA KARPO TRANSLATION COMMITTEE

Janson typeface with diacritical marks and
Tibetan Classic typeface
Designed and created by Tony Duff

First edition, December 2008
Second edition, February 2010
Third edition, September 2016
ISBN Paper: 978-9937-824-47-7
ISBN E-book: 978-9937-572-40-8

Produced, Printed, and Published by
Padma Karpo Translation Committee
P.O. Box 4443
Kathmandu
NEPAL

Committee members who worked on this book: translation and composition, Lama Tony Duff; cover design, Christopher Duff; editorial Lama Richard Roth.

Web-site and e-mail contact through:
http://www.pktc.org/pktc
or search Padma Karpo Translation Committee on the web.

Contents

Introduction v

From Longchen Nyingthig ཿ The Chod Practice Sound of Dakini Laughter ཿ by Jigmey Lingpa 1

Commentary on The Chod Practice Sound of Dakini Laughter 15

Profound Foremost Instructions for The Chod Practice Sound of Dakini Laughter by Dza Patrul Rinpoche 71

Glossary of Terms 95

Supports for Study 113

Tibetan Texts:

Jigmey Lingpa's Text 119

Dza Patrul's Text 130

Index 143

Introduction

This book is a compilation of materials needed for understanding and practising the Chod of the Longchen Nyingthig system of Great Completion dharma.

GREAT COMPLETION

The Great Completion system of dharma came from a land called Uddiyana, which these days is the Swat region of Pakistan. The name of Great Completion in the language of Uddiyana was "mahasandhi". The name mahasandhi means exactly "the great juncture" and refers to the one all encompassing space in which all that there could be—whether enlightened or unenlightened, whether belonging to nirvana or samsara—is present.

The Tibetans translated this name as "rdzogs pa chen po". The term "chen po" is the exact equivalent of "maha" and means "great" in English. The Tibetan term "rdzogs pa" is not exactly equivalent to "sandhi" because its literal meaning is "a state of completion" rather than "a juncture". However, the Tibetans chose "rdzog pa" to translate it in this case because one of the meanings of rdzogs pa, "a situation in which everything is present", matches the meaning of "sandhi". In the terminology of the original Tibetan translators, "chen po" is a literal translation and "rdzogs pa" is a meaning translation.

When this name is translated into English from the Uddiyanian term, it comes out to "Great Juncture" in both literal and meaning styles of translation. However, when translated from the Tibetan term, it comes out to "Great Completion" in literal translation and "Great Juncture" in meaning translation. Although the English translation "Great Completion" is used these days because of following the Tibetan wording literally, I think we should start using "Great Juncture" because it both translates the term literally and conveys the meaning intended. Nonetheless, for this book I have continued to use "Great Completion" in order to avoid confusion.

Arriving at a correct translation of the name like this is not done merely as an exercise in translation. It is done to bring out the great meaning embodied in the name. Great Completion refers to an all-inclusive space that beings including humans could realize. It is also used to refer to the system of instruction designed to bring them to an all-inclusive realization of that space. When a being does realize it, there is nothing more to be realized or done because all is complete within that being's space of realization and the work of spiritual practice is complete. In a Buddhist way of talking, Great Completion is the final realization in which that being has manifested true and complete buddhahood.

Great Completion is often called "Great Perfection" in English but "Great Perfection" presents an incorrect understanding of the original name. The final space of realization is not a state of perfection but one that contains both perfection and imperfection. The translation of the original term should not connect us to the idea of perfection but to the idea of the juncture of all things perfect and imperfect, that is, to the idea of a state of realization in which all things are complete. There is a second problem with "Great Perfection" that it feeds into the theistic habits of the West. It easily misleads people into thinking that it means a godly state of perfection.

I had the fortune to work for many years under the incomparable vidyadhara Chogyam Trungpa Rinpoche as a member of his translation committee. He was very alert to problems of translation and the effects of theism, and did not accept "Great Perfection" for the reasons given above. As a matter of interest, he preferred to use another name for Great Completion, "maha ati"[1], which is derived from the practice aspect of the teaching. By doing so, he emphasized the practical aspect of the teaching while avoiding the various problems that come with calling it "Great Perfection".

You might ask what the "great" in the name means. It does not mean that this is a "fantastic" or "wonderful" state of completion, a meaning that comes to many people based on the slang use of "great". In the Buddhist tantras, this term is used to distinguish something known by wisdom in direct perception from the same thing known by dualistic mind as a concept . In other words, *Great* Completion does not refer to the lesser state of completion understood through the use of concept but to the *great* version of that, the actual state of completion known through wisdom.

Nyingthig Great Completion

The Great Completion teaching is the ultimate of all Buddhist teachings though it has within it several, increasingly profound levels of teaching. The most profound level of teaching has an Indian name which literally says "heart's drop" but means "quintessential". It was translated into Tibetan as "nyingthig"[2] which also literally says "heart's drop" but means "quintessential". Thus,

---

[1] Tib. shin tu rnal 'byor. Meaning, "the ultimate of yogic practices". Sometimes it is written as "Maha Ati" to make the pronunciation clearer.

[2] Tib. snying gi thig le. The word "thig le" is also written in Tibetan as "tig le" with no difference in meaning.

Nyingthig Great Completion is the name for the quintessential level of Great Completion teaching.

LONGCHEN RABJAM'S TRADITION OF NYINGTHIG GREAT COMPLETION

The Nyingthig or quintessential level of Great Completion teaching had several lines of transmission within Tibet. The one called "Longchen Nyingthig" is a transmission of the Nyingthig teaching which came through the Tibetan master Longchen Rabjam [1308–1363][3].

Longchen Rabjam transmitted the teaching to Jigmey Lingpa [1730–1798] in a series of visions. Jigmey Lingpa in turn transmitted it to many disciples. One was his very close disciple Jigmey Gyalway Nyugu, some of whose disciples, such as Dza Patrul, have become famous as principal upholders of the lineage.

The story of the transmission of Longchen Nyingthig begins with Jigmey Lingpa. At one point in his life, Jigmey Lingpa went into strict retreat near Samye Chimpu, and practised the guru yoga of Longchen Rabjam for a long time. In 1759, at the age of 31, he stayed in two, different caves which had been named the Nyang Caves after Nyang Tingdzin Zangpo who had practised in them long before. It was in those two caves that Jigmey Lingpa met Longchenpa's wisdom body in a series of three visions. The first vision occurred in the Upper Cave of Nyang and the two later

---

[3] The Tibetan term "longchen" literally means "the vast space of a realized mind". This has sometimes resulted in the idea that "Longchen Nyingthig" means "the quintessential Great Completion that is like a vast space", but it is clearly explained in the Longchen Nyingthig tradition that the "Longchen" in Longchen Nyingthig is the first part of Longchen Rabjam's name and that Longchen Nyingthig means Longchen Rabjam's Nyingthig.

visions in the Lower Cave of Nyang. Jigmey Lingpa later named the lower cave Flower Cave of Great Secrecy.

The following description of Jigmey Lingpa's three visions was given by the late Tulku Urgyen and translated by Andreas Kretschmar. It is a condensation of Jigmey Lingpa's own record of his visionary experiences called *The Water Moon Dancer, The Story of the Realizations that Appeared as Very Secret Experiences.*

> On the 16th day of the eighth month, after I had composed a praise to this great and holy practice place, while sleeping in a state of unchanging luminosity, ordinary fixations on the five sense objects were purified and rough object fixations dissolved into the ocean-like consciousness. In this non-conceptual state of the alaya, the interdependent arising of phenomena subsided and the apparent luminosity of luminosity, rigpa wisdom arose.
>
> In this mirror-like state, I saw the glorious master from Samye, the all-knowing Lord of Speech, like a magical apparition. His noble body was beautified with the threefold monk's robes and he was a little advanced in age. Like with the Buddha, one could see no imperfection in him.
>
> I heard him say in a clear voice, "May the mind transmission of the meaning be transferred to you! May it be transferred! May you perfect the transmission of words! May you perfect it!"
>
> At that moment an unbearable faith and devotion, similar to falling unconscious, was born in me and without wasting time to prostrate, I immediately grabbed both hands of the All-knowing Lord and placed him on top of my head, the Great Bliss Chakra. Almost fainting

with devotion, I prayed to him, "All-knowing Dharma King, think of me! All-knowing Dharma King, think of me! All-knowing Dharma King, think of me!"

He replied, "I knew that in later times someone saying this would come". When I came back to my senses, I understood this to be an unhappy statement because when he was still dwelling in his physical body, beings of lesser merit had no faith and devotion toward him, and through the power of their bad practice they had brought sadness to his mind.

I said to him, "Thinking of your great kindness and how you benefited the dharma and beings with your Seven Treasuries[4] and the mind treasure of the Nyingthig alone, I have a constant devotion, seeing your outstanding qualities to be equal to those of buddha in person."

He looked straight at me and said, "Son of noble family! Now I have transferred the realization of the transmission of meaning to you by means of aspiration and entrustment. Erect the life-fortress of practice and teach extensively to the destined ones! And, your songs are excellent". As he said that, I thought of asking him for teachings but the vision of the three kayas dissolved like a magical apparition into the expanse[5].

After that, I thought unceasingly of the All-knowing Lord: "I would have thought that, for a poor beggar yogin like me, who practises in caves and is young in

---

[4] This is Longchen Rabjam's famous exposition of Great Completion, written as seven treasuries of profound dharma.

[5] See the glossary.

age, such realization would be impossible. However, just by seeing your face, all my latencies, negativity, and obscurations are gone. Just by hearing your voice, the great expanse of realization has burst forth and, without having studied the words of the teaching but merely by seeing the writings, I understand all the key points of instruction. In one day, your kindness has transformed me from a sentient being into an enlightened one."

Thus I was blessed with the transmission of meaning through various symbolic methods: outwardly through the tamer of beings, the Great Humkara; internally through the master Manjushrimitra; and secretly through the dharmakaya of Longchenpa. This was the first vision, in which I was blessed with his body.

At that time, I stayed in Nyang Tingdzin Zangpo's practice cave, which in the old guide books to holy places is referred to as the Upper Cave of Nyang. It is an overhang type of cave and now, to the right side of the entrance there is a white bush growing out of a crack in the rock and on the side of the rock are the outlines of three stupas, and the grass on the floor of the rock is moved by a continuous breeze.

People of former generations have written about the southern cave, also known as the Lower Cave of Nyang, as the Nyang cave. Through a vision, I gained confidence in what was previously written about it and remembered it to be the practice cave of the Dharma King Trisong Deutsen and Nyang Tingdzin Zangpo. Therefore, I gave the Lower Cave of Nyang the name Flower Cave of Great Secrecy.

While I stayed in this holy place in very strict retreat, I felt strong renunciation in my mind and had a vision in which all concretized dualistic fixation collapsed. I met the All-knowing One, the second buddha, Longchenpa, again. This time, he gave me a book with one chapter and said, 'In this, all the hidden points of the *Great Chariot* are clarified'. At that time, he taught the anthology of *Unravelling the Symbols of the Great Secret Treasury*.

Again he said, "This is a record of your former lives and predictions for the future", and handed me a scroll. When I opened it, I found that it contained two lines, one above and one below. The upper one read, "In your previous life, you were the All-knowing Dharma Lord[6]". As I began to read the lower one, the vision faded out like a cloud within space. At the time of this vision, I had no gross fixations that would think, "His body shape is like this or that". Thus he blessed me with his speech and I received the authorization to compose writings. This was the second vision.

After a few months, I met the All-Knowing Lord again. He was magnificent, wearing the robe of a pandita. He had the body of a very youthful man aged twenty. On his head, he was wearing the pandita hat with long flaps. With the mandala of his body and through the symbolic union of the five spontaneously-existing male and female buddhas, he conferred the empowerment of infinite luminous purity upon me. Without saying anything at all and with a kind and joyous smile, the wisdom vision of great purity dissolved into the expanse. Thus he blessed me with his mind and I received authorization as a master who has realized the transmission of actual meaning. This was the third vision.

---

[6] … meaning Longchenpa.

> At that time, my perception of objects became liberated, freed of all reference points, and my realization during meditation was without any restrictions. Internally, I was freed from the dualistic mind stream and therefore, everything was purified into limitless natural liberation. In my post-meditative wisdom perception, I spent the time in a happy yet saddened state of mind. With devotion and powerful longing, I composed the praise to Longchenpa called the Longing Song of the Spring Queen.
>
> The meaning of Longchenpa's *Three Chariots* and *Seven Treasuries* arose in my heart and I wrote many instructions concerning key points, quintessential teachings on view and meditation, and the essentials of practice. All were written in an easy-to-understand way with an economy of words, for example, *Words of the Omniscient One*, *White Lotus*, *Annihilating Deviations*, and so forth.

Jigmey Lingpa was not learned at all before having these visions but the realization transmitted in them opened his mind fully and he was able to write brilliantly afterwards. He wrote extensively on many subjects and, as part of his writings, made a complete record of the stories of the three visions and all of the dharma that he received directly from Longchen Rabjam's mind. All of his writings were later assembled into his *Collected Works*, with the texts that recorded the Longchen Nyingthig transmission taking up three volumes. These three volumes have since become known as *The Root Volumes of Longchen Nyingthig*. Late in the twentieth century, Dilgo Khyentse Rinpoche compiled two more volumes of important works written by later masters of the Longchen Nyingthig system and added them to *The Root Volumes*.

The original mind treasures included a short but complete set of instructions for Chod practice at the Nyingthig level of Great Completion. The instructions together with a liturgy for practice were written down in a text called *From Longchen Nyingthig: The Chod Practice Sound of Dakini Laughter*.

Chod as given in this text was, and still is, widely practised by followers of Longchen Nyingthig. For example, Dza Patrul [1808–1887], one of the very early holders of the lineage, practised this Chod and wrote a text containing profound, foremost instructions on the practice. His text is widely used as the source of instructions on how to do the visualizations of the practice and is included in this book.

A Summary of Chod

Chod practice itself is not part of the Great Completion system. It is the practice that goes with another system of dharma called "Pacifier Chod". The system of dharma called Pacifier Chod was brought into Tibet by Phadampa Sangyay who taught it especially to Machig Labdron and her son.

The system of dharma called Pacifier Chod gets its name from the fact that it *pacifies* or alleviates the sufferings of samsaric existence. Alleviating the sufferings of samsaric existence is the aim of all Buddhist teaching. Chod, which literally means to cut and here means to sever and eliminate, takes the specific approach of using yogic conduct to provoke upheavals of samsaric mind which are then used as fuel for abruptly severing their root, grasping at a self. Therefore, yogic conduct is a major theme of Pacifier Chod practice. One of the main features of the yogic conduct of Chod is to cast aside attachment to the body then offer the body as food for any being who wants to take it. Therefore, "casting aside the body as food" as it is called is also a major theme of the practice. The upheavals are deliberately brought on and the offer of body is made to troublesome spirits of varying kinds, primarily to what are called "gods, demons, and dons[7]", so they too are a major theme of the practice.

Nyingthig Chod and Pacifier Chod

Chod practice in the Longchen Nyingthig system has its own flavour and has quite a different feeling from Chod practice as it is normally done in the Pacifier Chod system. This is because of a difference in how the view is presented and practised in the two systems. It results in a different approach to the practice and different degree of emphasis on the yogic conduct connected with the practice.

Pacifier Chod is Vajra Vehicle dharma; it has the key point of empowerment followed by the practice of a deity, and does use the terminology of the Vajra Vehicle when discussing the view. However, it is strongly tied to the sutra vehicle's Prajnaparamita teaching of the view and generally presents the view in terms of ultimate Prajnaparamita, the space of direct experience of the mother or consort of the buddhas. The direct experience of ultimate Prajnaparamita is the same as the direct experience of alpha purity in Great Completion but the teachings of ultimate Prajnaparamita are much more path oriented than the teachings of the view presented in Great Completion. The teaching of view in Pacifier Chod starts with the concept of a problem that needs to be severed and ends up with the fact of the direct experience of Prajnaparamita, whereas the teaching of view in Great Completion bypasses concept all together and goes directly to the overarching expanse of that view.

This difference in presentation of the view affects the style of the practice. The practice of Pacifier Chod is deeply involved with various forms of yogic conduct and is very elaborate in style. In

---

[7] Tib. gdon. See the glossary.

contrast, Chod practice done within a true environment of Longchen Nyingthig teaching has little emphasis on the yogic conduct of Chod; it is very unelaborate in style. To put it in a more personal way, Chod practitioners are the sort who love the yogic lifestyle with all of its elaborate ways and unconventional behaviour. They like to blow on their thigh bone trumpets, play tunes on the large drum of Chod, think of practising in fearsome places in their small tents, and generally do all of the other types of unconventional, yogic behaviour that, taken together, constitute the world of the Chod practitioner.

The approach of the Nyingthig practitioner is different. The Nyingthig practitioner first and foremost practises Thorough Cut and Direct Crossing[8], the two practices that constitute the main practice of the system. After that, the Nyingthig practitioner might —or might not—do the Chod practice of the Nyingthig system as an ancillary to these two main practices. I have asked my teachers in Tibet about this and they have always replied that there is a practice of Chod in Longchen Nyingthig and that, as lineage holders, they are bound to present the practice but that for someone who really is a Nyingthig practitioner, the only thing to practise, if it suits the person, is Thorough Cut and Direct Crossing. Thus, in the Chod practice of Longchen Nyingthig, although one could go to terrifying places such as charnel grounds and could get fully involved with the elaborate yogic discipline of Pacifier Chod, that is not usually done. Some Longchen Nyingthig followers would not even bother with the Chod.

Thus, for the Nyingthig practitioner, the view is all important and the practice of Chod is a secondary teaching that can be included in it or not. I am connected with one of the main monasteries in Eastern Tibet that upholds the teaching of Longchen Nyingthig and have spent much time there receiving teachings and practising them.

---

[8] Tib. khregs chod, thod rgal. Thregcho, Thogal.

When we do Chod, we assemble as a group, use our thighbone trumpets and Chod damarus, but do not do much yogic conduct other than that. No-one bothers with having a khatvanga or any of the many other ritual implements that are part of general Chod practice. Rather, the space of Nyingthig Great Completion realization is always the main point and we do the practice of Chod within that. To do it, we use the text that Jigmey Lingpa received from the wisdom dakinis and which is presented in this book.

There is a difference between the practice of Chod and the practice of Longchen Nyingthig Chod as I have experienced it in Tibet and Nepal. I have discussed this with a number of lineage holders and they agree that the difference lies in how the space of realization is presented and on how much emphasis it is given. Of course, if you talk with a Pacifier Chod practitioner, he will agree that the factual, actual[9], lived space[10] of mother Prajnaparamita is the key point.

---

[9] This means the one which is not the fiction known by concept but the actual, superfactual one known by wisdom in the direct perception of emptiness. Also see superfactual in the glossary.

[10] Tib. nam mkha', dbyings, and klong correspond to "space", "expanse", and "lived space". They are important terms in tantric literature and especially in Great Completion. All have the general meaning of space but each has a specific and important connotation. When they are all translated as "space", which frequently happens, crucial meaning is lost. The first term listed simply means space. This term is not used much in this book but when it does appear, it is written simply as "space". The second term means an expanse of space, for example in the "space-like expanse of emptiness". It indicates experience of a vast, empty expanse and is often a synonym for emptiness. It is always translated as "expanse" in this book. The third term, and the one footnoted here, is often used in this book. It has the specific sense of a space that one is in the midst of and experiencing on the spot. An example given for this space is that it is like the space experienced by a parachutist. It is more than an experience of expanse. It is the

(continued ...)

However, there is a significant difference between the expression of that view in the usual presentation of Chod and in the Longchen Nyingthig system.

As mentioned above, the view of the Longchen Nyingthig system is the most fruitional view available to humans on this planet whereas the view of Pacifier Chod is more path oriented. Moreover, the style of Nyingthig dharma in general is to cast aside pre-occupation with elaborate practices that are meant to lead to the view and to enter the view directly and in a very unelaborate way, whereas the style of Pacifier Chod is to make yogic discipline the very means by which one enters the view. There is an example that shows the difference between the style of Great Completion dharma and Pacifier Chod that also succinctly shows the difference between these two approaches to Chod. It is the difference between the garuda bird who has already learned to live in space and who just swoops down and carries off the whole poisonous shrub of samsara and the peacock who eats the poisonous shrub, thrives on it, and slowly becomes more magnificent as he does.

All of this is beautifully summed up in the opening lines of Jigmey Lingpa's Chod text:

> Nature Great Completion ░
> Cuts at the root to a single sphere ░
> Therefore it transcends cutter and cut ░
> But there are people who are elaborate in style and ░
> Who would make a path of the conduct of yogic
>   activity, ░

---

[10] (... continued)
experience of space all around that is filled with its own specific type of experience. For example, parachuting over a city will be a different lived experience of space from parachuting over a forest. Each lived space has its own specific content. I have always translated it as "lived space" in this book.

> Therefore I show the foremost instructions for casting
> aside the body as food. ༔

Here is a paraphrase of these lines done as a word by word commentary, with the words of the text shown in italics.

In other words, a practitioner whose wants a practice which is totally concerned with the luminosity nature of his own mind might take up the practice of *Great Completion*. Great Completion is also called *Nature* Great Completion because the focus of the practice is luminosity, also called the nature[11]. Someone who does take up this practice will put his effort into the practice of Thorough *Cut*, which cuts *at the* very *root* of the problem, grasping at a self. Using the profound foremost instructions of the Thorough Cut system, he will return to the *single sphere* which is the lived space of realization in which everything is included, that is, Great Completion or Dzogchen.

Because the teaching of Great Completion is the approach to practice which simply bypasses all lesser types of practice in which there is still some conceptual orientation, a practitioner of Great Completion *transcends* any ideas of a *cutter* that would cut at the root of the problem *and* the root of the problem that would be *cut* by it. The name "Chod" means "cut" so the words here are not only pointing out the style in general of Great Completion practice but are also making a play on the word "Chod". In other words, this is also saying that a practitioner of Great Completion bypasses lesser forms of practice such as Pacifier Chod in which there is still a concept of cutter and object to be cut.

However, even amongst people who follow the Nyingthig teaching there will be those who cannot just stay with the ultimate simplicity of the overarching space of Thorough Cut practice but need some

---

[11] An explanation of Nature Great Completion is given on page 21.

complexity with it. *There are* these *people who* need a more *elaborate style* of practice and some of them are people *who would make a path of the conduct of yogic activity*, meaning that they would do the Pacifier Chod type of practice. *Therefore*, because there are such people even amongst Nyingthig practitioners, *I*, Jigmey Lingpa, *show the foremost instructions for casting aside the body as food.* The phrase "casting aside the body as food" explained briefly above is part of the terminology of the Pacifier Chod system. Again, it refers to one of the main practices of Pacifier Chod in which there is the two-fold meaning that the practitioner first casts aside all cares for his body and second offers it to the gods and demons as food for them to take.

All in all, these few words of Jigmey Lingpa at the beginning of the Longchen Nyingthig Chod text show the view of the Nyingthig system of Great Completion and how the Chod practice could be joined with it.

The Chod Text of Longchen Nyingthig: "Chod Practice Sound of Dakini Laughter"

The text for Longchen Nyingthig Chod came as part of the mind treasures received by Jigmey Lingpa from Longchen Rabjam. It is both the basis for the Longchen Nyingthig style of Chod and the liturgy for doing the practice. As such, it forms the basis of this book.

The translation of the text started life in 2007, when Chris Vicevich contacted me, asking for a new translation of the text. The first step in translating a text is to obtain a reliable edition of the Tibetan text. Two well-accepted editions of the Tibetan text are available at the moment; one was made by Shechen Monastery in Bauddha, Kathmandu at the command of Dilgo Khyentse and one by the current Dodrupchen in Sikkim. Both were made in the latter half of the twentieth century based on what is regarded as the best edition available before that, the one made in Tibet by Adzom Drukpa. We looked at both editions and some other copies whose original source was unknown. We found that the Shechen Monastery edition was the best, though we found some minor errors in it. We investigated the text with various lineage holders both outside and inside Tibet and, based on their replies, were able to produce a corrected edition of the text which we believe to be truly error free. This new edition has been included in this book.

I would like to thank Lama Wangdu here for his help. He is regarded amongst Tibetans—including the Dalai Lama who has taken teachings from him—as one of the greatest Chod masters in Asia at the moment. When we were preparing the corrected Tibetan text, he was always able to explain what should be the correct rendering. He was even able to point out that a particular wording in the Shechen edition, one which has been altered in all other editions, was correct. He encouraged the work of a fresh translation and provided several more clarifications to Jigmey Lingpa's text.

Commentary to the Liturgy

Jigmey Lingpa's text has the unusual quality so often found in revealed treasures of the Nyingma tradition of having few words but exceptionally clear meaning. Nonetheless, it does require explanation. Therefore and with the encouragement of various people including Lama Wangdu and also the senior khenpo of the monastery I am affiliated with in Tibet, I wrote a commentary to explain the text.

The commentary is what is called a "bit-wise" commentary in Tibetan circles. This kind of commentary does not proceed word by word but first examines the text to find those bits that need explanation—whether words, phrases, or whole sections of the text—then explains their meaning.

In the commentary, I have given a few hints about the meaning of Great Completion as it applies to this practice. However, as with all commentaries on these matters, it can only be a support for explanations of the profound details of the practice obtained in person from one's own guru.

Commentary to the Liturgy by Dza Patrul

Neither the text itself nor my own commentary to it give much detail about the visualization procedures of the practice. Therefore, a text about that is needed by anyone wanting to do the practice. Dza Patrul, who is one of the principal early lineage holders of Longchen Nyingthig and who wrote many commentaries for Longchen Nyingthig practice, wrote such a text. It is called *Profound Foremost Instructions for the Chod Practice Sound of Dakini Laughter*. I recently stayed with Khenpo Dralha, the head instructor of the retreat centre of Dzogchen Monastery in Tibet and he was kind enough to privately teach me Patrul Rinpoche's entire commentary. Dzogchen Monastery is one of the main centres for the Longchen Nyingthig teaching in Tibet so the khenpo was able not only to teach me the words of this Chod system but to successfully transmit the "feel" of the Nyingthig approach to Chod, which has made its way into this book. My great thanks go to him on behalf of all of us!

Dza Patrul's text is included in his *Collected Works* and I used an original print of the woodblock edition of the collected works made by the Derge Printing House. The Derge edition has mistakes in it, therefore I corrected them and made the new edition available at the end of this book.

The text is a text about visualization procedures but, as its name suggests, it is more than that; it is a text which shows the inner meaning of the practice and in doing so shows the visualization procedures in detail. Although there are other commentaries to

Jigmey Lingpa's text, this is the one that is generally used these days when the details of the visualization procedures need to be understood.

USING THE TEXT AS A PRACTICE TEXT

Jigmey Lingpa's text includes and is used as the practice text. The English translation presented in this book is the practice text for English speakers. For those who are able to practise in Tibetan, the Tibetan text is the practice text.

I am genuinely sorry that I could not provide practice texts in French, German, Italian, or the many other languages in which a practice text is needed. As someone who has been deeply involved in the transmission of Tibetan Buddhism to the West for many years and whose experience with practitioners runs across a remarkable number of countries, I do not see a need for the type of text in which there is a line of Tibetan text, followed by a line of transliteration, then a line of translation. I firmly believe that we should do our practices in a language in which we are fluent whether it be English, French, German, Tibetan, or some other language. This does not mean that we should abandon the Tibetan text; there is great value in studying the source text in order to be really sure of what it says, and that was the prime reason for providing the Tibetan text in this book. The point that I am making is that we should be looking ahead and moving towards providing and even composing practice texts in our own languages. The provision of an all-English version of the practice text here is consistent with that ideal.

The text proceeds in a linear sequence and is easy to use as a practice text. Unlike with some other texts, there is no need to move backwards and forwards or add inserts when it is being used as a practice text.

The Tibetan practice text needs clarification and so does the one in English. To provide for that, every place that might need explanation has been clarified in one of the commentaries or in the glossary in this book. There is a graded approach to this: my own commentary comes immediately after the liturgy to give a general explanation of the practice and to clarify terms; Dza Patrul's commentary following that gives profound instruction on the practice; and the glossary comes last.

Significant portions of the text are to be chanted. The text uses several Tibetan literary devices to fill these sections with the rhythm that is so important to Chod practice. Much of this was lost in other translations but I have managed to get most of it into English. Some of the lines of the text compress a lot of meaning into a very short space which means that these lines come out quite long in English. I did my best to make these lines amenable to rhythm, but always followed the principle of not eliminating any meaning for the sake of making some lines shorter or easier to chant. Anyone wanting to use the translation as a practice text could, once the meaning contained in the lines has been understood, shorten them, according to need. In the end, we will have to write our own practices in English and other languages and put them together with verse or rhythm that really works for us. In the meantime, we do the best we can, and some experimentation is in order.

Tibetan verse has a fixed number of syllables per line which makes it easy to construct certain types of melody for chanting. European languages do not work like that, so from the start we should abandon attachment to tunes from the past and try to come up with tunes that fit our present situation. For example, it is very possible to use certain types of English chanting or singing that fit with the energy of Chod practice. This does make the verses, as I have translated them, very alive. While I was staying in the magic forest at Broceliande in France, where I first translated this text, I went into the forest and sang many songs of this type in Gaelic style to the gods and demons who inhabit that place. It worked very well! I can tell you that we do have Western ways of singing that fit with the assured bravery of the Chod yogic discipline and which really do work with the text as translated here. As the vidyadhara Chogyam Trungpa, a great champion of this kind of thought often said to his students, you can do it! Please experiment and make your own tunes in your own language; it can be done and can be done very effectively.

Points of Style

In general, the style of translation throughout this book is very accurate. Long sentences are standard in Tibetan and we have kept them where possible. Even the idiom of the various authors has been rendered into English. Thus, if there is something unclear in the English or a long or unusual turn of phrase, you can be sure that it was there in the original. Also, the texts here use a great deal of specialized terminology including the unique terminology of Great Completion and much of it is not well known. However, none of it has been glossed over and that means that there will be new terms or new ways of expressing terms. As mentioned above, there has been a concerted effort to ensure that everything that might need clarification has been explained.

Then there is the point that I have often abandoned the use of the more formal English "one" in favour of the less formal but much more personal "you". Decades of experience have shown me that this is the tone of Tibetan texts and also that this is how the mind of a practitioner works. Accordingly, texts connected with practice like the ones in this book should be translated with the more personal "you" even if it is the less formal style of English composition. My thoughts on this have been proved by the many practitioners who have come and thanked me for taking this approach because, as they have said, this style of composition is very personal and goes straight to the heart.

In Tibetan texts, procedural remarks, notes, and the like are written in smaller lettering to distinguish them from the main text. I have used the English convention of setting such text in italics.

Finally, note that Tibetan writing uses a specific punctuation mark to show breaks. The usual form is simply a vertical stroke. However, that is replaced in revealed treasure texts with a variant called a "revealed treasure mark" which looks like this ༔ though it is written like this ༔ in Jigmey Lingpa's revealed treasures. During the 1980's the Nalanda Translation Committee was translating revealed treasures and discussed their work with Dilgo Khyentse Rinpoche who was visiting at the time. He said that it was important to retain the revealed treasure marks because they immediately and definitely indicate to the reader that the text is revealed treasure. Accordingly, all revealed treasure marks that appear in the original Tibetan texts are shown in the English texts.

The use of revealed treasure break marks has another useful aspect. Many Tibetan texts contain a mixture of both revealed treasure and ordinary text. The use of revealed treasure marks in these texts not only identifies the revealed treasure text but also distinguishes it from the rest of the text. The Tibetan edition of Jigmey Lingpa's text does have a few short notes that were inserted after the treasure was revealed. Their normal Tibetan punctuation distinguishes them from the revealed treasure portions of the text that come with have revealed treasure break marks.

About Sanskrit

Sanskrit terminology is properly transliterated into English with the use of diacritical marks. However, these marks often cause discomfort to less scholarly readers and can distance them from the work. Padma Karpo Translation Committee's intent was to publish a book which would not only set a high standard for presentation of this material in English but which would also be widely used. Therefore we made the decision to use Sanskrit diacriticals with mantras and syllables only where it is needed to clearly distinguish the words involved. Some people might be dissatisfied by this choice; we apologise to them in this time when such issues of translation are still being worked out.

Further Study

Padma Karpo Translation Committee has amassed a wide range of materials to help those who are studying this and related topics. Please see the chapter "Supports for Study" at the end of the book for all the details.

Health Warning

This book is about a subject that is generally kept secret. There are various reasons for that, not the least of which is that you could harm yourself by trying to engage in these practices without personal guidance from a qualified teacher. In Tibet, books like this have always been in regular use but are only ever used as a support for teaching received in person from someone respected as a capable guide. Thus, if you have not heard these teachings in person from someone who you respect and can follow, it would be best not to read them and certainly not to try to practise them. These days there are both non-Tibetans and Tibetans in many countries who can give you the teaching and guidance needed to use what is contained within this book.

In sum, the contents of this book could be dangerous to your spiritual health if you are not ready for what it contains, so please exercise care.

Best wishes to all of you.
May you accomplish the practice of Chod!

Tony Duff,
Swayambunath,
Nepal,
December 2009

Plate 1. Wall mural at Dzogchen Monastery, East Tibet, Showing Jigmey Lingpa, picture by the author, 2007.

From Longchen Nyingthig ꞉
The Chod Practice

Sound of Dakini Laughter ꞉
by Jigmey Lingpa

I prostrate to the lady queen of the expanse, great bliss, Yeshe Tshogyal. ꞉

Nature Great Completion ꞉
Cuts at the root to a single sphere ꞉
Therefore it transcends cutter and cut ꞉
But there are people who are elaborate in style and ꞉
Who would make a path of the conduct of yogic activity, ꞉
Therefore I show the foremost instructions for casting aside the body as food. ꞉

The requisite articles are as follows: ꞉
For subjugating the haughty ones, ꞉
The skin of a carnivorous beast with the four clawed feet intact; ꞉
For the view pitched from above, a small tent; ꞉
For the conduct ascending from below, a khatvanga; ꞉
For bringing the gods and demons under your control, a great supreme thighbone trumpet; ꞉
For subjugating appearances, a damaru; ꞉
For governing the host of mothers, bells, little bells, ꞉
And chevrons of hair made with tiger and leopard tufts. ꞉

In short, the items appropriate to the yogic activity ꞉
Are the preparation that is to be made. ꞉

Then, in a place that gives a terrifying impression, ꞉
Rather than taking a condescending stance towards the gods and demons, ꞉
Or being driven by thoughts of the eight worldly concerns, ꞉
Use the four immeasurables to rouse an attitude of bravery. ꞉
Appearances are to be taken charge of as soon as they appear; ꞉
Not to adjust them right then with the subjugating visualization ꞉
Would be equivalent to giving in to the enemy. ꞉
Therefore, with rigpa, yogic activity, and ꞉
A "PHAṬ", send from your heart centre ꞉
A nine-pointed vajra of meteoric iron, ꞉
An unyielding, hefty and solid mass ꞉
Blazing with light and flames, ꞉
Down onto that terrifying place, like a lightning bolt. ꞉
Think that the gods and demons dwelling there with their hordes, ꞉
Powerless to run away and scatter, ꞉
Stay there, their will to fight broken. ꞉
Then, abandoning pretense, shyness, and so on— ꞉
The hesitations of ordinary people—and ꞉
With a strong assurance of yogic activity, ꞉
Go, from amongst the four ways of going, ꞉
In the strong manner of assurance of the view. ꞉

Further, think this. The gods and demons of appearance and becoming, ꞉
The dons having an abode there, and demons of the road, all of them roaming about ꞉
Are summoned together and, like herding goats and sheep, ꞉
Are helplessly penned into that terrifying place. ꞉
As soon as they have been put in there, ꞉
Assuming the stance of blazing savagery, ꞉
Take all the gods and demons by their feet, ꞉

Swing them around three times overhead, ꞉
Then smash them down onto the solid ground. ꞉
Toss aside your small tent and mat. ꞉
No matter how composed the gods and demons might be, ꞉
Unable to stay unaffected, they will become upset. ꞉
If your yogic discipline is weak, ꞉
Apply this to your mind gradually. ꞉

Then, I create myself instantly ꞉
As the secret wisdom dakini ꞉
Equal in size to the entire universe, ꞉
Her body complete in every respect. ꞉
Loudly blowing the human thighbone trumpet, ꞉
I rouse the force of the view and perform the dance. ꞉

PHAṬ ꞉
I, a yogin with the conduct of fearless yogic activity, ꞉
Use the conduct of a mind equally encompassing samsara and nirvana ꞉
To dance upon the gods and demons of self-grasping ꞉
And smash dualistic thinking, samsara's discursive thought, into dust. ꞉

Root and lineage vidyadhara gurus, come to the dance! ꞉
Ocean of yidam heros, come to the dance! ꞉
Host of dakinis who scout the places, come to the dance! ꞉
Grant your blessings so yogic activity turns into the path! ꞉

PHAṬ ꞉
Dancing now on the eastern continent Purvavideha, ꞉
Where the dance floor of the dakas and dakinis is a circle round, ꞉
I dance up and down on the head of anger, Gyalpo, and ꞉
Trill, trill, trill, the flute of mirror-like wisdom. ꞉ HŪṂ HŪṂ HŪṂ ꞉

PHAṬ ༔
Dancing now on the southern continent Jambudvipa, ༔
Where the dance floor of the dakas and dakinis is a triangle pointed[12], ༔
I dance up and down on the head of arrogance, Lord of Death, and ༔
Thwack, thwack, thwack the skull drum of wisdom of equality. ༔ HŪṂ HŪṂ HŪṂ ༔

PHAṬ ༔
Dancing now on the western continent Godaniya, ༔
Where the dance floor of the dakas and dakinis is a semi-circle round, ༔
I dance up and down on the head of desire, Rakshashi, and ༔
Ting, ting, ting, the bells and little bells of discriminating wisdom. ༔ HŪṂ HŪṂ HŪṂ ༔

PHAṬ ༔
Dancing now on the northern continent Uttarakuru, ༔
Where the dance floor of the dakas and dakinis is a square around, ༔
I dance up and down on the head of jealousy, Samaya-breaker, and ༔
Flap, flap, flap the chevrons of all-accomplishing wisdom. ༔ HŪṂ HŪṂ HŪṂ ༔

PHAṬ ༔
When dancing on the peak of central Meru, ༔

---

[12] Normally the shape of the southern direction, in keeping with the enriching quality of the ratna family, should be a square, and the shape of the northern direction, in keeping with the destroying quality of the karma family, should be a triangle. Dza Patrul's commentary on the practice states it to be so, though revealed treasures sometimes change things away from the unexpected.

Where the dance floor of the dakas and dakinis is so majestic, ꞉
I dance up and down on the head of ignorance, Death Demon, and ꞉
Sing, sing, sing the HŪṂ song of dharmadhatu wisdom. ꞉ HŪṂ HŪṂ HŪṂ ꞉

PHAṬ ꞉

Saying that, dance, maintaining awareness without focus. ꞉
Then, pitch a small tent: ꞉
Visualize that you drive stakes of meteoric iron ꞉
Into the limbs of the malevolent gods and demons ꞉
Of that ground, who have fallen supine on their backs. ꞉

PHAṬ ꞉
Vajra dakini in the east ꞉
Carries the stake of great loving kindness. ꞉
Ratna dakini in the south ꞉
Carries the stake of great compassion. ꞉
Padma dakini in the west ꞉
Carries the stake of great joy. ꞉
Karma dakini in the north ꞉
Carries the stake of great equanimity. ꞉
Buddha dakini in the centre ꞉
Carries the stake of enlightenment mind. ꞉
They drive them into the heads and four segments ꞉
Of the gods and demons of self-grasping ꞉
Fixing them so that they cannot move. ꞉
PHAṬ ꞉

Say that and enter equipoise that does not reference ꞉
The three of self, other, and gods and demons. ꞉
Following that, identify the demons again and ꞉
Engage in the actual giving of the body. ꞉

PHAṬ ꞉
In the expanse of self-appearances, luminosity-great bliss, ꞉

The space divorced from the elaborations of conceptual effort and activity, ༔
The root guru, the sixth one Vajradhara, ༔
The mind, symbol, and aural lineage gurus, yidam deities, ༔
Dakinis, dharmapalas, and guards massed like clouds, ༔
Are visible, unstopped, in the midst of a sphere of rainbow light. ༔

With that, visualize the accumulation field and ༔
Think that you lead all sentient beings, with gods and demons ༔
Put foremost, in taking fully-informed refuge. ༔

PHAṬ ༔
Because of not knowing that this uncontrived, ༔
Self-arising rigpa is the entity of the objects of refuge, ༔
Beings are drowning in the ocean of suffering— ༔
Please give them refuge with your mind of the three kayas. ༔

Repeat that three times then arouse the mind: ༔

PHAṬ ༔
The mind that grasps at appearances as things ༔
Is totally severed by the conduct of yogic activity ༔
Then in order to realize the actuality of reality ༔
I arouse the mind freed from hope and fear. ༔

Repeat that three times. Then offer a mandala, thinking that your torso is Mt. Meru, your limbs the four continents, your fingers and toes the sub-continents, your head the god abodes, your two eyes the sun and moon, and your inner organs the wealth of gods and men: ༔

PHAṬ ༔
Self-cherishing's aggregate, this illusory body, ༔
Is fully arranged as the heaps of a mandala ༔
Then offered without expectation to the deities of the accumulation field. ༔
May the root of self-grasping be cut! ༔
PHAṬ ༔

Then, guru yoga: ༔

PHAṬ ꞉

In the expanse without outflows, dharmakaya's space, ꞉
Amidst its lustre, a sphere of intermeshing rainbow rays, ꞉
Is the father, knower of all the three times, Padmasambhava, ꞉
In the manner of a heruka whose conduct is yogic activity, ꞉
Together with an ocean of mother dakinis assembled. ꞉
Your body with the sparkling marks and signs is a lamp alight, alight. ꞉
Your speech with dharma for those to be tamed is sounding, resounding. ꞉
Your mind the state of luminosity, is the vajra essence. ꞉
Your son supplicates you with intense devotion. ꞉
Outwardly, the gods and demons' form is discursive thought risen up as an enemy; ꞉
Inwardly, hope and fear is the mind grasping at duality; ꞉
In between, various appearances are all the unfavourable conditions— ꞉
May the profound dharma, Cutter of Mara, ꞉
Cut them off right now, on this very seat! ꞉
So that the conqueror's level, expanse dharmakaya be seized, ꞉
Father, revered guru, please grant your blessings! ꞉
PHAṬ PHAṬ PHAṬ ꞉

Say that and dissolve the accumulation field into yourself. ꞉
Enter into equipoise of the non-dual state. ꞉

PHAṬ ꞉

Then this impure portion, the body of latencies, ꞉
So gross due to being very well fed and fattened, ꞉
Has the pure portion, rigpa, brought out from within ꞉
In the form of the Wrathful Woman, with the sound of PHAṬ! ꞉

Having one face, two arms, flaying knife and skull cup, ꞉
She slices the skull off my body. ꞉
Spanning the thousandfold realm ꞉

It is placed on a hearth of three skulls and inside ꞉
The body of elements set out as the feast is made ꞉
By the light of the three syllables to blaze into amrita. ꞉
OṂ ĀḤ HŪṂ and HA HOḤ HRĪḤ ꞉

The more you recite them, the more it is purified, increased, and transformed. ꞉
For the multicoloured distribution, that is developed ꞉
Further into all things which are desirable to mind— ꞉
Productive forests, food, clothing, medicine, and so forth. ꞉
For the red distribution, the Black Wrathful Woman ꞉
Flays the skin from your own impure-portion body, ꞉
Spreads it out to span the third-order thousandfold world, ꞉
Piles bodies, flesh, and blood into a heap on top, ꞉
And you think of it as a slaughterhouse. ꞉
For the black distribution, think that all diseases and dons, ꞉
Evil deeds and obscurations, accumulated beginninglessly ꞉
By sentient beings, yourself and others, condense into ꞉
A black cloud that dissolves into the heap of bodies ꞉
And the gods and demons devour it, making their ꞉
Bodies turn black like charcoal. ꞉
Call out to the guests of the offering and generosity like this: ꞉

PHAṬ ꞉
You the recipients of offering, the three roots and samaya'd ones, ꞉
Then you the recipients of generosity, principally of the eight classes of elementals, ꞉
Up through the demons and dons of retribution, ꞉
Come to this place of yogic activity's conduct! ꞉

Today, I the fearless yogin ꞉
Arrange this illusory body that parts samsara and nirvana ꞉
In a kapala having the area of a third order world ꞉
As the feast offering of the grand lifeless corpse. ꞉
I transform it into amṛita of un-outflowed wisdom. ꞉

This magical display that appears as the ninefold wishes ꞉
Offered without the grasping of self-cherishing ꞉
Is a grand feast indeed, please come as the guests! ꞉
Oh the sound of the great supreme skull drum so bright! ꞉
Oh the melody of the great grounds' trumpet so sweet! ꞉
Oh the flash of the bells, little bells, and chevrons so delightful! ꞉
Just like vultures flocking to flesh, ꞉
Please come here, this instant! ꞉
PHAṬ ꞉

Then there is the offering and dedication: ꞉
PHAṬ ꞉
To the vidyadhara gurus of the Three Lineages ꞉
Starting with the primordial protector ꞉
And going through to the root guru, ꞉
And to the yidams, dakinis, and dharma protectors, ꞉
I make the offering of the amṛita of the grand lifeless corpse. ꞉
May I and others, with gods and demons brought to the fore, ꞉
Complete the two accumulations and purify the two obscurations. ꞉
Due to taking yogic activity to its end for the benefit of migrators, ꞉
May appearances be trained into luminosity-illusion and ꞉
Dread and anxiety be liberated into dharmakaya. ꞉
Please bless me to be heruka in style. ꞉

PHAṬ ꞉
To the eight classes of elementals, to the non-humans ꞉
Who have transcended this world and who have not, ꞉
And to the host of flesh-eating dons who lead beings astray, ꞉
I offer on top of a human hide spanning the third order ꞉
Thousandfold world heaps of flesh, blood, and bones. ꞉
If I grasp at a self, oh how weak I am! ꞉
If you cannot do it, you are even worse! ꞉
If you want it now, swallow the raw flesh whole! ꞉

If you have no hurry, cook it in chunks and eat it! ꞉
Don't leave behind even a speck! ꞉

PHAṬ ꞉
For those who from beginningless time in samsara ꞉
Have retributions resulting from murderous grudges, ꞉
And those who just came by for the leftovers, guests of my compassion, ꞉
And every one of those who is menial and has no say, ꞉
I dedicate an inexhaustible treasure of desirable objects ꞉
Of the senses, according to whatever you individually want! ꞉
May all connected to me, both good and bad, become buddhas ꞉
And be cleansed of their debts of retribution. ꞉
PHAṬ ꞉

Saying that, give without reservation. ꞉
Enter into equipoise in the state of emptiness. ꞉
At that point, if you have self-cherishing for body ꞉
And fearful hesitation appears in mind, ꞉
Rouse assurance with the thought, ꞉
"The body, having been given to the gods and demons, is gone ꞉
And mind is free of ground and root— ꞉
Let alone the demons, even the buddhas do not see it", and ꞉
Decide firmly that what comes up in mind is your own face. ꞉
There are maras that have physical substance (note in text: outer conditions such as the elements, wild beasts, violent men, and so on, and the discursive thoughts of attachment, anger, and so on) and maras that do not (note in text: internal conditions such as mind's moods of happiness and sadness, and so on) ꞉
Maras of outer enjoyments (note in text: thinking only of yourself; the conceit of being concerned with one's own happiness, and so on) and maras of holier than though attitudes (note in text: doubt, hesitation, and so on). ꞉
Exclaim PHAṬ *and sever them in the expanse!* ꞉
Further, to show the timings: ꞉

In the early dawn period, in order to complete the two accumulations ༔
The white distribution is done to increase the amṛita substance; ༔
At mid-day, in order to purify retributions ༔
Dedicate the multicoloured distribution where suitable; ༔
In the evening, in order to rouse the path of yogic activity ༔
Perform the red distribution to totally sever grasping at a self; ༔
In the early night, to purify evil deeds do the black distribution. ༔
All of these involve transformation of your outlook, ༔
So the main thing is to practise by doing the visualization. ༔
At that time, no matter what trickery of illusion occurs, ༔
Adjust it with the view freed of temporary experience. ༔
If the degree of expanse with the yoga is small and ༔
The storm of what is provoked is difficult to adjust or ༔
The gods and demons, having a greater expanse, are not provoked, ༔
You should do the visualization of the white skeleton. ༔
Saying "PHAṬ", instantly I become ༔
A white skeleton, blazing with fire. ༔
A fire arises from its enormous size that ༔
Incinerates the thousandfold world and ༔
Particularly the dwelling place of the gods and demons. ༔
Finally, the skeleton together with the fire ༔
Turns to light and vanishes, and you stay in the state of emptiness. ༔
This practice is particularly effective at giving protection against contagious disease. ༔

If signs of completion of the practice do not arise in a timely way, ༔
And malevolent demons target you for violence, ༔
Make your rigpa evident in the form of the Wrathful Woman ༔
And think that she flays the skin from your impure-portion body ༔
And makes it into a human skin covering the three thousandfold world. ༔
She lays a carpet of flesh and bones out on top of it ༔
Which the demons and obstructors indeed long to devour. ༔
At that moment, Wrathful Lady gathers up the human skin all at once, ༔

Ties it with a lasso of snakes and intestines, ༔
Whirls it overhead and smashes it down, ༔
Making pulp of their flesh and bones. ༔
Many emanation wild beasts consume it, ༔
Leaving nothing. ༔
Mix expanse and rigpa, and enter equipoise. ༔
Certainty of completing the practice will arise and ༔
The violence of the demons and dons will have been eliminated; ༔
The rational mind that grasps everything with self-cherishing having been abandoned, ༔
Everything will be cherished by assurance of the view. ༔
At that time, signs of: provocation like finishing, ༔
Finishing like provocation; ༔
And also a mixture of both; ༔
And latencies like both; ༔
And finishing and provocation both finalized; ༔
Will be the temporary experiences that come from doing the conduct. ༔
It is when you have entered the space in actual fact ༔
Of the mind of selflessness, Samantabhadri, ༔
The great mother Prajnaparamita,
That the Cutter's Object will have come about as the path. ༔ ***SAMAYA*** ༔

In conclusion, the prayers of dedication and aspiration: ༔

AḤ
When the mass of concepts, virtuous and unvirtuous, is self-liberated, ༔
The concept labels of hope and fear are not referenced ༔
But the infallible interdependency of the appearing factor, the continuity of the mass of virtue, ༔
Has to be dedicated within the un-outflowed dharmadhatu. ༔

PHAṬ ꞉

Through the generosity of the fictional body ꞉
May those with debts of retribution accumulated over kalpas have them purified and ꞉
When their mindstreams have been liberated by the truth of superfactual dharma, ꞉
May they appear as the first ones in my assembly. ꞉
At that time, when the uncontrived, self-present, innate fact ꞉
Has been produced in the mindstreams of the unruly gods and demons, ꞉
Instead of following after the confusion of grasping at "I", ꞉
May their mindstreams be moistened with love and compassion. ꞉
And for myself, having taken the conduct of yogic activity to completion, ꞉
May happiness and sadness have their taste equalized with samsara and nirvana trained into dharmakaya. ꞉
May I be victorious in all directions with every connection that I make a meaningful one, ꞉
And may I take enlightened activity to completion and accomplish a rainbow body! ꞉

PHAṬ ꞉

Say that, while preserving the lustre in the state of the view. ꞉
Placing importance on great compassion, ꞉
Do the visualization of sending and taking (note in text: sending my own happiness to the gods and demons and taking the gods and demons suffering onto myself) happiness and suffering, ꞉
And do totally pure generosity (note in text: that is, say these expressions of auspiciousness: "All dharmas arise from causes …" and, "Do no evil deeds whatsoever …" and "May those spirits left here still …") of dharma. ꞉
Make positive relations and obstructive connections, good and bad, into the path of emancipation. ꞉

SAMAYA ꞉ MA MA KO LING SAMANTA ꞉

These are the thighbone trumpet melodies:

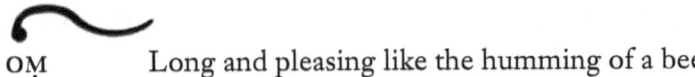

OṂ Long and pleasing like the humming of a bee.

HŪṂ Powerful and dignified like the neighing of a horse.

TRĀṂ Wrathful and cruel like the roar of a tigress.

HRĪḤ Moving and vibrating like the voices of gandharvas.

ĀḤ Moving and vibrating like the last one above, but rising up at the end with what is called "the whistle of the dakinis".

Author's Commentary to "The Chod Practice Sound of Dakini Laughter"

Title

The title says, "From Longchen Nyingthig: ཿ The Chod Practice Sound of Dakini Laughter ཿ "

As is often done with a dharma teaching that has a number of texts associated with it, the title of this text begins by indicating the name of the dharma teaching from which the text is drawn. This text is drawn from the collection of texts that comprise the writings of Longchen Nyingthig so the title begins literally with the words, *From Longchen Nyingthig:* .

As explained in the introduction, Nyingthig is a name for the level of Great Completion[13] teaching that is above all other levels of teaching including other Great Completion teachings. Of the various Nyingthig teachings that appeared in Tibet, this is the one that came from Longchen Rabjam so it is called "Longchen Nyingthig".

That is followed by the actual title of the text *The Chod Practice Sound of Dakini Laughter*. To understand the title, we first have to understand that the word "Chod" literally means "the act of cut-

[13] Tib. rdzogs pa chen po. Dzogpa Chenpo or Dzogchen.

ting". When it is used as the name of a dharma practice, it has the specific sense of severing and elimination. What is to be severed and eliminated by the practice of Chod is the four maras[14] because the teachings of Chod identify them as the representatives of all possible forms of neurosis.

The first part of the title "Chod Practice" is a Tibetan term which has two, similar meanings[15]. The first meaning is object of the cutting, that is, the place where a cut is to be made. According to that, the first part of the title could be understood to mean the object or target of the cutting done in the practice of Chod, which would be the four maras. The second meaning is arena of cutting. According to that, the title would mean the overall situation in which the cut was being performed, in other words, the practice of Chod itself.

It is very common for Tibetans who have a general knowledge of Chod to think that the first words of the title have the first meaning. However, lineage gurus of the Longchen Nyingthig have unanimously explained to me that the words of the title have the second meaning. Thus, the first part of the title does not mean "Object of Chod practice, the four maras" but means "Chod practice in general".

---

[14] The explanation that the object of cutting is the four maras is very much the style of explanation of the general system of Chod. Commentaries written from the Nyingthig perspective will often cut right to the heart of the matter and state that the object of cutting is the self that is clung to by ignorance—that, after all, is the root from which all maras come. The meaning is ultimately the same, but the difference in explanation does reflect a difference of approach to practice, as mentioned in the introduction.

[15] Tib. gcod yul.

The second part of the title is "Sound of Dakini Laughter"[16]. It is very easy to misunderstand the Tibetan term that corresponds to "Sound of Laughter"[17]. The term is made up of two words that seem to be saying that the dakinis are laughing loud or long and this has resulted in Tibetans and Western translators alike thinking that it means "roar of laughter", "loud laughter", "bellowing laughter", and the like. However, the two words together have a specific meaning which cannot be guessed at by looking at the individual meanings of the words. The two together refer to the general noise made when one or more people laugh. For example, a group of people in a room are amusing themselves with laughter and a person outside hears it as a buzz of laughter; the buzz or general sound of laughter reaching the other person is what is being referred to here.

Given the possibilities mentioned so far, one idea put forward by Tibetans and Western translators alike for the title is that it means "the dakinis are roaring with laughter at the maras who are the object that will be cut down by this practice of Cutting". For example, it is explained this way in a well-known Tibetan commentary to this text called *Store of the Dakini's Secret, An Excellent Vase of Amṛita* written by a disciple of Tshogdrug Rangdrol. Generally speaking, that commentary is excellent and because of that I have used it and referred to it later on in this commentary, but it does make a mistake here. The title does not mean that the wisdom dakinis are jeering or derisively roaring with laughter at the object of cutting, the maras. One of the key points of Chod is that you do not take a condescending attitude towards the negativities invoked in the practice. This point is made very strongly by Dza Patrul in the advice and also in the poetry near the end of his commentary *Profound Foremost Instructions for the Chod Practice Sound of Dakini Laughter*. This is an example of how understanding mistaken

[16] Tib. mkha' 'gro gad rgyangs.

[17] Tib. gad rgyangs.

interpretations of the text can help to deepen our understanding of Chod.

Every lineage-holding guru of this practice of Chod with whom I spoke explained to me that the title cannot be understood through the literal meaning of its words but has to be understood as follows. There are both worldly and beyond-worldly dakinis. Of them, it is the beyond-worldly or wisdom dakinis who voice the message of blissful wisdom to the practitioner. The messages might start out in the wisdom space of these dakinis as their amusement which is the meaning of "laughter" in the title but there is no telling how their message will manifest in this world. It could be as human speech, for example when Tilopa heard the dharmakaya speaking the hearing lineage Vajrayogini tantras from the middle of the sky. It could be as sounds of giggling laughter which is spoken of in Vajra Vehicle texts and which I have heard on several occasions; it is very distinctive. It could be as strange sounds that convey meaning to a particular person. For Jigmey Lingpa, what appeared to be the sounds of crows cawing was in fact the sounds of the wisdom dakinis tittering away, communicating the meaning and also the tunes of Chod to him. What he heard unravelled itself in his mind—a mind which had been fully blessed and made capable of doing so by Longchen Rabjam—as the text here and the tunes of Longchen Nyingthig Chod that go with it. That is how the words "Sounds of Dakini Laughter" in the title have to be understood.

Lama Wangdu pointed out to me that the word "sound" in the title, a word that literally means "drawn out" or "long", could also be taken to mean the "drawn out" cadences of the sounds that Jigmey Lingpa heard and which became the cadences of the tunes that he put with the text that he wrote down. He demonstrated the sounds, which are long and drawn out melodies for the Chod liturgy.

The title, like the body of the text, is not punctuated with normal punctuation marks but with revealed treasure break-marks (༔).

These are put there to show that this text really did come as a direct communication from the dharmakaya, via the wisdom dakinis, which is the essence of what the title is getting at.

We can now put together the whole title. It is one long title that contains this meaning: "The Chod Practice which is the Sounds of Dakini Laughter that were heard by Jigmey Lingpa then decoded and written down by him". Note that, while most translations show the text as having the title "Chod Practice" with a sub-title of "Sounds of Dakini Laughter" that is not the case. Rather, the title is just one long title embodying the meaning given.

Now Nyingthig Chod is different in some ways, as was mentioned in the introduction, from general Chod. There is a strong emphasis within the Nyingthig teachings on dharmakaya and the world of a Nyingthig practitioner is very much about that. Thus, the sound of dakini laughter is not something that happened only for Jigmey Lingpa, but is very much something that can happen to us, as practitioners, too. In this regard, a number of very experienced Chod practitioners have said to me that the messages coming from the wisdom dakinis often do come as sounds within the environment which a good practitioner can pick up on. Therefore, the title of the text is reminding us practitioners that the dharmakaya can bleed through into the environment of our world. It is telling us that there are messages that come through into our world when the wisdom dakinis are communicating with us.

In sum, there is Chod practice and there has been and continues to be communication from the wisdom dakinis about how that is to be done and how the maras are to be cut by it. This communication came to Jigmey Lingpa in the form of sound and it has come to others in various ways and it could come to us, too. And that is the meaning of the title.

PREFACE

First comes the homage. The text says,

> *I prostrate to the lady queen of the expanse, great bliss, Yeshe Tshogyal.* ꞉

Yeshe Tshogyal, the consort of Padmasambhava, represents the feminine principle which is the space of emptiness known by prajna.

A point to note throughout this and other tantric texts is that, "emptiness", which is very dry, is usually replaced by "expanse" which conveys the space-like experience of emptiness. You will see it in many places in the text and should understand it as an experiential word for emptiness.

Yeshe Tshogyal is a "queen of the expanse" which in the Tibetan words of the text literally means a woman who has mastery over the expanse. Expanse is not just nothing but also everything and when the expanse is coming out into appearance, a person who has mastery of the expanse experiences its appearances as great bliss. That is the literal meaning of the words of the homage. However, the sequence of the words also contains meaning, which is that she has mastered the expanse and because of that experiences appearance as great bliss.

After the homage comes the declaration of composition, which shows the reason for writing the text. It says:

> *Nature Great Completion* ꞉
> *Cuts at the root to a single sphere* ꞉
> *Therefore it transcends cutter and cut* ꞉
> *But there are people who are elaborate in style and* ꞉
> *Who would make a path of the conduct of yogic activity,* ꞉

Therefore I show the foremost instructions for casting aside the body as food. ༔

Nature Great Completion is one of the several, special names for Great Completion. This name is not "natural great completion" nor "the true nature Great Completion" which are incorrect for two reasons. In terms of grammar, the first term is the noun "nature" not the adjective "natural". In terms of meaning, the noun nature is used because it refers to the nature aspect in particular of the three characteristics of the essence of mind—entity, nature, and unstopped compassionate activity—used to describe profound reality as experienced by the practitioner. Thus, this name is not intended to refer in any way to Great Completion being a "natural" practice or being connected with a "natural reality" or any of the many other, incorrect meanings that arise from the mistaken wording "natural Great Completion".

The next two lines are a play on the name of Chod which, as mentioned before, means "Cutting". Nature Great Completion cuts to a single unique sphere of reality that embraces everything. Therefore it is a practice that transcends all concepts of a cutter and something to be cut. Moreover, this cut is not done either gradually or with the use of any elaborate style of practice. Rather, Nature Great Completion cuts at the root meaning that it cuts, right at the earliest possible place and on the spot, to reality. Because of that Nature Great Completion is not an elaborate style of practice.

Ordinary people do have conceptual elaborations made up by dualistic mind, such as the ideas of cutter and the thing cut. Of the ones who follow a path of dharma, some prefer to practise in the simpler style of Nature Great Completion just mentioned and some prefer a more elaborate style of practice. Of the ones who prefer a more elaborate style of practice, some like to engage in the special types of conduct involved with yogic activity of one sort or another and prefer to make that into a path back to the single unique sphere of reality. For the sake of these ones who with their preference for elaboration would make a path out of the particular type of yogic conduct that involves casting aside the body, the author declares that he will write the text to give them the foremost instructions[18] needed for this particular practice.

"Yogic activity"[19] is a general name for certain types of behaviour or conduct used by yogi types on their journey to enlightenment. The Tibetan name does not mean "crazy wisdom" or "mahasiddha activity" but simply means yogic behaviour used as a path to enlightenment.

Body of the Text

The text says,

> *The requisite articles are as follows:* ༔
> *For subjugating the haughty ones,* ༔
> *The skin of a carnivorous beast with the four clawed feet*
> *intact;* ༔
> *For the view pitched from above, a small tent;* ༔
> *For the conduct ascending from below, a khatvanga;* ༔
> *For bringing the gods and demons under your control, a great*
> *supreme thighbone trumpet;* ༔
> *For subjugating appearances, a damaru;* ༔
> *For governing the host of mothers, bells, little bells,* ༔
> *And chevrons of hair made with tiger and leopard tufts.* ༔
> *In short, the items appropriate to the yogic activity* ༔
> *Constitute the preparations to be made.* ༔

This practice of Chod is a deity practice. In general, deity practice is elaborate in style and has a preparation phase that is followed by

---

[18] See the glossary.

[19] Tib. brtul zhugs.

the actual practice of the deity. Jigmey Lingpa starts by explaining the preparation phase which he says for this practice consists of gathering the articles needed for the practice.

The practice centres on cutting the maras connected with the appearance of gods and demons. Various, specific articles are used during the performance of the yogic activity done for that purpose. Each article has a symbolic meaning which is mentioned here.

First, for subjugating the "haughty ones", a particular skin is needed. All the details of the skin are fully and correctly mentioned in this translation. "Haughty ones" is a general name given to troublesome gods and demons; they have a very high opinion of themselves and are usually troublesome because of it. The meaning of "haughty ones" is very similar to the modern American slang "someone with an attitude".

The mention of haughty ones brings us to a discussion of what is called subjugation. Chod practice has a number of themes and practices corresponding to those themes. The haughty ones is a major theme and the main practice connected with them is subjugation. The meaning and importance of the practice of subjugation is shown very clearly in Dza Patrul's commentary.

Chod practice uses the haughty gods and demons to achieve its goal of enlightenment by deliberately provoking them to begin with. The provocation has the one purpose of causing seeds of negativity in the practitioner's mind to be popped, like pimples, in what are called "upheavals". The practitioner has to provoke the upheavals first then deal with them second. The teaching of Chod shows the practitioner how to deal with them in a way that will lead to enlightenment. The main way to deal with them is through subjugation. In essence, that is the practice of Chod.

There are three main subjugations in Chod practice. Grasping at a self, the place of the practice, and the gods and demons in the place of practice are the three things to be subjugated. The Tibetan term for subjugation[20] literally means to overwhelm something or someone with one's greater brilliance. In Chod, the dark idea of a self, the general degradation of samsara represented by the gods and demons, and the fearsome practice location which is the abode of the gods and demons all are overwhelmed with the brilliance of non-self in particular and the goodness of buddha dharma in general. The result is that the three are outshone and brought under one's power; they are subjugated.

The three subjugations are done in various ways throughout the practice and there are specific visualizations connected with them. These are called the subjugating visualizations. Again, Dza Patrul's commentary makes this aspect of the practice very clear.

Returning to the items needed for the practice, next there are two things that go as a pair.

> *For the view pitched from above, a small tent;* ꞉
> *For the conduct ascending from below, a khatvanga* ꞉

The view is brought down from above into the practice like pitching a tent; a tent is erected above and fastened to the ground below. The tent is a small tent, a Tibetan-style, one man tent, which is tall and not very wide, and not like the low and long kind of "one-man tent" seen in the West. This tent symbolizes the view in Chod being brought down from above and fastened to the conduct so that the conduct is encompassed by it. The tent also symbolizes the conduct in Chod being used to lead the practitioner up from below into the view, like climbing a mountain. The conduct in the case of Chod is the yogic activity specific to the practice of Chod. A Chod

---

[20] Tib. zil gyis rnon pa.

practitioner has a khatvanga as a general symbol of being a person who does yogic activity type of practice.

The meaning of the lines concerning the thighbone trumpet and damaru should be clear. However, there is a point to be made here. In tantric language, there are a number of special terms for real, human articles. One of them is "great". For example, a "great supreme" thighbone trumpet means one obtained from a human corpse. Great is used later in the text, as are a number of other code words, to indicate human parts.

The "bells" and "little bells" mentioned here and in other places further in the text are symbolic of maintaining control of the dakinis. Note that dakini is a very wide ranging term, covering many different types of beings and principles, from very samsaric to very enlightened. There are two types of bell involved; both are small in size but one is smaller than the other. These bells were worn in ancient India and still worn today by Indian woman in order to be attractive. For example, an Indian woman's anklets have the little bells on them and her wristlets have the (slightly larger) bells on them.

Then the text instructs which place to use for the practice:

> *Then, in a place that gives a terrifying impression,* ༔

A particular type of place is needed to do Chod and the Chod practitioner is told to travel to such places to do the practice; the type of place needed is one that provokes upheavals in the mind.

The main texts of Chod explain very clearly that "a place that gives a terrifying impression" really means "a place inhabited by gods and demons".

The term "gods and demons" is used consistently throughout the instructions of Chod, so it is important to understand it. It refers overall to spirits who are haughty and have the attitude that they will use their power to get the better of and possibly even harm anyone who comes into their place. Within this, "gods" refers in general to spirits who come from the levels higher than humans and "demons" to those who come from the preta realm, which is lower than the human realm. Note that there are two sorts of pretas. The first sort is constantly hungry and thirsty and does have any ability to interact with other beings. The second sort, and the sort being referred to here, can interact with beings in the human realm and often have the ability to manipulate the form of the human realm. The second sort includes all the ghosts, apparitions, and spirits who at very least will play tricks on humans and at very worst can cause serious harm to humans. "Demons" refers to this second kind of being. Essentially, they are what Western culture thinks of as evil spirits and ghosts of all kinds.

The best place for Chod practice is one in which there really are gods and demons who have the ability to make trouble for you. If you can go to that kind of place, the gods and demons will not merely be a projection of your own mind but will be beings in their own right who are not friendly and who do have the ability to affect your mind and environment. Because of that, they really can create the conditions needed for strong Chod practice. If such a place is not available, at very least you need to find a place which has an eery feeling to it, one that makes your skin crawl if possible. The presence of beings in such a place might be your projection but because those kinds of projections do come in that particular place, it too provides the right circumstances for Chod practice.

Someone has referred to these as "power places" but that does not go far enough. Some power places are very nice places that do not cause major upheavals in the mind of anyone who visits them and that is not what is being referred to here. As mentioned above, the term really means "a place of dangerous beings" and refers to places inhabited by malicious gods and demons. Again, the texts of Chod clearly state that such places are needed because they allow upheavals to be provoked in the mind of the practitioner, upheavals which then become the very basis for Chod practice.

It should probably be pointed out that there is a tendency in Western cultures to disbelieve or at least downplay the idea of spirits. Because of it, some Westerners might want to downplay the idea of a spirit-filled place. However, the teaching of Chod clearly states that Chod is about dealing with both external and internal demons. It says that the best practice is done in places where there really are other beings whose presence can provoke upheavals in your mind.

Now, having gone to a place suited to the practice, you start the practice by rousing the right attitude. The text instructs which attitude to rouse for the practice:

> *Rather than taking a condescending stance towards the gods and demons,* ༔
> *Or being driven by thoughts of the eight worldly concerns,* ༔
> *Use the four immeasurables to rouse an attitude of bravery.* ༔

The exact wording of the Tibetan text of the first line is that the attitude to develop is "not a condescending one in which you feel how good you are compared to the gods and demons and how much stronger you are than them". Unfortunately, that is a mouthful for one line, so I have tried to shorten it down without losing too much of the meaning.

The next line says that your attitude also should not be driven by the eight worldly concerns. For example, the practice should not be done for purposes of fame or personal gain. Rather, your motivation should be the enlightenment mind[21], that is bodhichitta, which in the Chod tradition is developed through the four immeasurables.

[21] See the glossary.

The last two lines presented the attitudes needed for all practices of enlightenment in general. The next lines explain the attitude needed for Chod practice in particular. This attitude of bravery is connected with subjugation of the gods and demons. The text says,

Appearances are to be taken charge of as soon as they appear; ꞉
Not to adjust them right then with the subjugating visualization ꞉
Would be equivalent to giving in to the enemy. ꞉

Specifically, the attitude of brave assurance is needed in order to do the subjugations. Brave assurance is the confident air that one actually can subjugate the gods and demons. It is the bravery of a warrior who has no second thoughts; it is not stupid fearlessness based on a hardened idea of self. It is the assurance of a practitioner who knows he can liberate the outbursts of mind on the spot; it is not the assurance of a person who tells himself he can do it but has no ability with the mind.

For beginners, this has to be aroused as best as possible. As the realization of absence of self develops, it will form the basis of true fearlessness which is at the root of bravery. As the practice develops there will be confidence followed by assurance that liberation of the output of mind can be done because of one's realization.

All in all, there has to be a warrior-like brilliance based not on the idea that the gods and demons are nuisances and have to be crushed but that one can fearlessly subjugate them and the whole situation. That comes initially from some understanding of goodness and later from realization of absence of self.

A correct understanding of the words here is fundamental to understanding the practice of Chod. The Tibetan to begin with here could be understood literally to be saying "Appearances are to be crushed". However, that would mistake the meaning and possibly cause a serious mis-understanding of subjugation and how it has to be practised. The paragraph here is stating one of the fundaments of Chod practice, which is that your job as the practitioner is to be in control of appearance from the outset. The first line says that you must stay on top of appearances when they do happen rather than letting them get the upper hand. The second line says that, if needed, you must adjust them. This word "adjust" is used a few times in the text; it is a term that means to tune something so that it now works for the practice, like tuning a radio so that a station which before was ragged and unclear now comes in according to the needs of the listener. You have to stay on top of the appearances and then, if some appearances need it, you do not crush or mutilate them but adjust them, with the adjustment always being one of bringing them back into line with reality.

In short, you keep the upper hand and make the appearances work for you. You do that using the specific, subjugating visualizations of the practice. In this type of practice it is either you or the appearances coming at you that will win out. Therefore, if you do not do the subjugation on the spot, it will be too late; you will have lost the battle to the appearance and that would be the same as giving in to the enemy.

Thus, with the attitude that you are going to take charge of appearance, you bring forth rigpa as your guru has shown you to do and mix the yogic activity of this particular practice with the rigpa. Joining the yogic activity of the practice with rigpa turns it into a liberating activity, and with that, you assert your control over the place of practice. You arouse true assurance of yogic activity by making sure that it is properly mixed with rigpa then, henceforth, conduct yourself at all times with that assurance. This "rigpa" is the key word of key words in Great Completion; it is often translated these days with "awareness" but that fails to capture the meaning of the term[22].

Therefore, with rigpa, yogic activity, and ༔
A "PHAṬ", send from your heart centre ༔
A nine-pointed vajra of meteoric iron, ༔
An unyielding, hefty and solid mass ༔
Blazing with light and flames, ༔
Down onto that terrifying place like a lightning bolt. ༔
Think that the gods and demons dwelling there with their hordes, ༔
Powerless to run away and scatter[23], ༔
Stay there, their will to fight broken. ༔
Then, abandoning pretense, shyness, and so on— ༔
The hesitations of ordinary people—and ༔
With a strong assurance of yogic activity, ༔
Go, from amongst the four ways of going, ༔
In the strong manner of assurance of the view. ༔

This section is called the phase of subjugation done before departing for the place of the gods and demons. Dza Patrul's commentary clearly explains this visualization. Meteoric iron needs some explanation; see the glossary. With this visualization, the practitioner rouses assurance of the view as the basis for doing whatever he does. Note that the text does not say "to go in the four ways with assurance of the view as the best", but says that "of the four ways that you could go about"—meaning four specific ways mentioned in Great Completion —you should "go with the assurance of the view".

---

[22] See rigpa in the glossary for more information.

[23] The Shechen edition of the Tibetan text has a mistake here and we have corrected it. The translation has been made according to the correction. See the Tibetan text included in this book for more information.

This term "assurance", which is used many times throughout the text, is very important. Assurance is different from confidence and the difference is a key point in Vajra Vehicle teaching[24].

Having developed this kind of assurance as the basis for all of your conduct, you summon up all the gods and demons and force them into that place, like herding animals into a pen.

> *Further, think this. The gods and demons of appearance and becoming,* ꞉
> *The dons having an abode there, and demons of the road, all of them roaming about* ꞉
> *Are summoned together and, like herding goats and sheep,* ꞉
> *Are helplessly penned into that terrifying place.* ꞉

The first two lines summon up all gods and demons possible. First, it mentions the ones of appearance and becoming[25]. "Appearance and becoming" is a general term for all the different types of abodes and beings there are, so the first line means all of them in general. The next line includes both the ones who live in the place of practice and all the others who are on the road, roaming in other places. The term "dons" is a general term for negative influences[26]. Here it is referring to the negative forces in general whose dwelling place is the terrifying place you have chosen for the practice.

All of them in the three groups just mentioned are free to do as they wish. In order to get them worked up, you capture them and bring them all into your place of practice, then pen them in. The image is like herding sheep into a pen; they are forced, helplessly, into the pen and squeezed in very tight. Note that the text says they are helplessly forced into the pen—this does not mean that they are

---

[24] See the glossary.

[25] For "appearance and becoming" see the glossary.

[26] Tib. gdon. See the glossary.

helpless once they are penned but means that they have no control over your capturing and penning them in.

Having penned them in like that, many of them will be upset. However, some might still be composed in their haughty way, thinking that they are on top of the situation. So now, to strongly provoke them:

> *As soon as they have been put in there,* ༔
> *Assuming the stance of blazing savagery,* ༔
> *Take all the gods and demons by their feet,* ༔
> *Swing them around three times overhead,* ༔
> *Then smash them down onto the solid ground.* ༔
> *Toss aside your small tent and mat.* ༔
> *No matter how composed the gods and demons might be,* ༔
> *Unable to stay unaffected, they will become upset.* ༔
> *If your yogic activity is weak,* ༔
> *Apply this to your mind gradually.* ༔

The text here is not talking about what to do upon your arrival, but is talking about what to do when you have brought all of them in and penned them there. You provoke them by picking them up, whirling them around, then hurling them to the ground. The ground is "hard ground" not "powerful ground", so you are swinging them around and smashing them down onto hard ground—ouch! That helps to get them upset. Tossing aside your tent, and so on, means that you uproot your tent and your sitting cushion in a wild fashion and toss them aside, which shows the gods and demons that you really mean business. No matter how unflappable these gods and demons might have been before, this will get them worked up.

This could be dangerous. If you really get them provoked, you will need great assurance of yogic activity mixed with rigpa, as discussed just before this, to be able to deal with it. This assurance is not a beginner's practice so, if you do not have great assurance of rigpa mixed with yogic activity, you must exercise care here. This is a very important point. You provoke gently at first then work your way up doing it very strongly.

Now that the mandala of the deity has been established, the next step is the self-visualization. The text says,

> Then, I create myself instantly ꞉
> As the secret wisdom dakini ꞉
> Equal in size to the entire universe, ꞉
> Her body complete in every respect. ꞉
> Loudly blowing the human thighbone trumpet, ꞉
> I rouse the force of the view and perform the dance. ꞉

The text does not say "forcefully generate the power of realization" but says to rouse the force of the view, which is a very different thing. The next verse is the actual rousing of the view in preparation for the dance:

> PHAṬ ꞉
> I, a yogin with the conduct of fearless yogic activity, ꞉
> Use the conduct of a mind equally encompassing samsara and nirvana, ꞉
> To dance upon the gods and demons of self-grasping, ꞉
> And smash dualistic thinking, samsara's discursive thought, into dust. ꞉

"Yogi" is a male term. Conveniently, "yogin" is a term that covers both men and women. You are a yogin of a practice that depends heavily on behaviour. The behaviour you depend on is the special, yogic activity of Chod. It involves a fearless kind of behaviour. However, this is not the fearless behaviour of an ordinary person; it is the behaviour of a person who has the view of Great Completion. When your mind has that view, it is a mind that extends equally throughout samsara and nirvana because samsara and nirvana are co-present in the space of realization. You are using that kind of mind that encompasses all of samsara and nirvana on the spot to dance up and down on the gods and demons produced by the mind that grasps mistakenly at a self.

Dualistic thinking is the general process of a mind involved with grasping at a self and it comes out as the various discursive thoughts of beings who are in samsara. The text does not say that it grinds that thought to dust but that it just smashes it to dust in one blow.

The Tibetan word for "dance" is not the same as the word "trample". Tibetan dance is a rather deliberate style of dance, with great emphasis on a downward stamping kind of movement. In fact, the word for dance in Tibetan implies that you are stomping as you dance. Altogether, the image here is of dancing up and down and trampling as you do.

Now that you are mentally prepared for the dance, you invite the enlightened guests of the dance—the three roots—and, once they are imagined to be there, ask for their blessing before starting the dance.

> Root and lineage vidyadhara gurus, come to the dance! ༔
> Ocean of yidam heros, come to the dance! ༔
> Host of dakinis who scout the places, come to the dance! ༔
> Grant your blessings so yogic activity turns into the
> path! ༔

"Dakinis who scout the places" is a way of talking about the many lesser dakinis who wander about the various places that there are, sacred and otherwise.

The next five verses cover the dance. The energies of the five buddha families, which are the enlightened aspects of the five main types of afflicted energy, are invoked one at a time. The Tibetan verses are written using special literary devices for developing a sense of rhythm and energy and they have been reflected as closely as possible in the English.

Tibetan verse has the great advantage of a fixed number of words per line, so melodies can easily be made to go with the verses. English does not work like that but it is possible to use certain types of English chanting or singing that fit with the energy of Chod practice and which make the verses very alive. Let's take just the first verse as an example:

> PHAṬ ༔
> Dancing now on the eastern continent Purvavideha, ༔
> Where the dance floor of the dakas and dakinis is a circle round, ༔
> I dance up and down on the head of anger, Gyalpo, and ༔
> Trill, trill, trill, the flute of mirror-like wisdom. ༔ HŪṂ HŪṂ HŪṂ ༔

The image is of a dance and dance floor. The dance floor in each case is the specific shape of the element, the afflicted energy, and the enlightened energy that goes with the direction of the verse. Here we are in the eastern continent of our Mt. Meru world system. That is our dance floor. The element corresponding to the eastern direction is water. The shape corresponding to that is a circle, though the Tibetan says it poetically, calling it a "circle round". You are dancing in the style of the wisdom dakini—who you now are—and with the Tibetan sense of dance mentioned above. You are not exactly stamping on the head of anger, the affliction connected with the east; you are "dancing on" this energy—you have subjugated it and do not take it so seriously. At the same time, you are jumping up and down on it with your yogic activity, so the text says, "dancing up and down".

Each verse mentions a specific personification of the afflicted energy you are dancing on. These personifications come from Indian culture and its perceptions of these energies. Gyalpo, meaning "king", is a type of spirit that is the personification of anger. The Lord of Death, Yamaraja, is connected with the failings of arrogance. This part here does not mean "the arrogant lord of death" but that arrogance is the affliction and the Lord of Death is the personification of it. Rakshasi is a fierce cannibal demon like the troll of European lore and is the personification of desire. Samaya-breaker[27] is a type of spirit connected with corruption of samaya and is a personification of jealousy. Death Demon is a type of spirit generally connected with the deadness of ignorance. Note that Death Demon is different from the more well-known Lord of the Dead who is master over the whole death and death process of sentient beings. Death Demon is more like "deadness demon", a personification of the quality of general ignorance.

You dance upon these energies and their personifications, some as gods and some as demons, and as you do, you display their respective enlightened aspects. The Tibetan here uses a special literary device that brings a great sense rhythm. Just reading the word puts you in the mood, so to speak. So, we "trill, trill, trill the flute of mirror-like wisdom", and so on. Each of the five wisdoms is invoked from the affliction and mentioned in its appropriate place. And, corresponding to the fact that wisdom has been invoked, HŪṂ HŪṂ HŪṂ follows because it is the primordial utterance of dharmakaya wisdom in general.

Note the progression within each verse. The PHAṬ to start with clears self-grasping. Then you, the wisdom dakini, do the dance in the appropriate place. You dance on and subjugate the affliction of that place. You enjoy it as its appropriate wisdom. You end by proclaiming the utterance of dharmakaya wisdom.

> PHAṬ ༔
> Dancing now on the southern continent Jambudvipa, ༔
> Where the dance floor of the dakas and dakinis is a
> triangle pointed, ༔

[27] Tib. dam sri.

I dance up and down on the head of arrogance, Lord of Death, and ꞉
Thwack, thwack, thwack the skull drum of wisdom of equality. ꞉ HŪṂ HŪṂ HŪṂ ꞉

PHAṬ ꞉
Dancing now on the western continent Godaniya, ꞉
Where the dance floor of the dakas and dakinis is a semicircle round, ꞉
I dance up and down on the head of desire, Rakshashi, and ꞉
Ting, ting, ting, the bells and little bells of discriminating wisdom. ꞉ HŪṂ HŪṂ HŪṂ ꞉

PHAṬ ꞉
Dancing now on the northern continent Uttarakuru, ꞉
Where the dance floor of the dakas and dakinis is a square around, ꞉
I dance up and down the head of jealousy, Samaya-breaker, and ꞉
Flap, flap, flap the chevrons of all-accomplishing wisdom. ꞉ HŪṂ HŪṂ HŪṂ ꞉

PHAṬ ꞉
When dancing on the peak of central Meru, ꞉
Where the dance floor of the dakas and dakinis is so majestic, ꞉
I dance up and down on the head of ignorance, Death Demon, and ꞉
Sing, sing, sing the HŪṂ song of dharmadhatu wisdom. ꞉ HŪṂ HŪṂ HŪṂ ꞉
PHAṬ ꞉

At the end of the dance the text says,

Saying that, dance, maintaining awareness without focus. ꞉

"Awareness" here does not mean "rigpa", but is a general term for conscious mind, enlightened or un-enlightened. "Focus" is a technical term for a concept that is taken as the current point of attention. Altogether, this means that you keep an awareness while you are dancing but without any conceptual ideas in it. That in turn means that you try to stay in rigpa.

You have danced on the gods and demons and subjugated them with the result that they are lying on their backs in their respective places. Next, you nail them down so that they are fixed in a powerless state. This is all done within the view and the view is symbolized by the small tent of a Chod practitioner so the tent is mentioned to start with:

> *Then, pitch a small tent:* ༔
> *Visualize that you drive stakes of meteoric iron* ༔
> *Into the limbs of the malevolent gods and demons* ༔
> *Of that ground, who have fallen supine on their backs.* ༔

This does not mean "pitch a tent on the ground of the cruel demon" but means to pitch a tent of the view which is done by nailing down self-grasping, as represented by the gods and demons, so that it no longer operates.

The word stake here translates the Indian term "kila" which was translated into Tibetan with "phurpa"[28]. Kila is a general term for any kind of sharp device used to nail or pin something down. It is then used as the name of the ritual implement used in this and other practices to symbolize overcoming affliction. Thus, stakes mentioned here and in the following lines could be understood as ritual

---

[28] Although this is often written as "phurba" in English, in fact the Tibetan spelling and pronunciation too is "phurpa".

phurpas made of meteoric iron[29] nevertheless they are functioning as stakes.

Each of the five wisdom dakinis uses a particular stake to nail down the gods and demons of self-grasping. The first four stakes are the four energies that lead to the development of enlightenment mind, the four immeasurables. They are mentioned in their order, and are followed by a fifth stake, the stake of enlightenment mind.

In the Indian and Tibetan tradition, the word "great" is used sometimes to indicate the real thing as opposed to a conceptual idea or description of it. Thus, each of the four immeasurables is called "great" here not because it is great in a general way but because it is actually manifest at this point. The four segments are the four limbs of the body. When the text says "carries", it means holds and brings the particular stake mentioned to the task.

> Vajra dakini in the east ꞉
> Carries the stake of great loving kindness. ꞉
> Ratna dakini in the south ꞉
> Carries the stake of great compassion. ꞉
> Padma dakini in the west ꞉
> Carries the stake of great joy. ꞉
> Karma dakini in the north ꞉
> Carries the stake of great equanimity. ꞉
> Buddha dakini in the centre ꞉
> Carries the stake of enlightenment mind. ꞉
> They drive them into the heads and four segments ꞉
> Of the gods and demons of self-grasping ꞉
> Fixing them so that they cannot move. ꞉
> PHAṬ ꞉

---

[29] Also, see meteoric iron in the glossary.

Next, the text says to enter non-referential meditation on emptiness in which there is no you as the wisdom dakini, nor others—gods and demons in this case—as the object.

> *Say that and enter equipoise that does not reference* ꞉
> *The three of self, other, and gods and demons.* ꞉
> *Following that, identify the demons again and* ꞉
> *Engage in the actual giving of the body.* ꞉

"Referencing" is a technical term of general Buddhism that means knowing something by referencing it with a concept instead of directly perceiving the actual thing. Thus, not referencing means not being involved in dualistic mind, with its concepts. In this case, it means to enter the equipoise of non-duality in which the concepts of oneself as the actor and of others as the ones acted on—especially the gods and demons—are not present.

Having done that, you arise into post-meditation and return to the state of mind in which there are concepts of the demons. The term "identify" is the technical term for using concepts to know something. A great deal could be said about this, because it is also possible to identify something, meaning that you can know it, without having self-grasping. In that case, you would enter the non-referential meditation on emptiness and then arise in rigpa which was knowing the content of the rigpa. That is just a hint at the profound meaning hidden in these words. Your guru could explain it further. This is in fact what is being said, as can be seen in the next part below. It is part of the special teaching of Great Completion in relation to Chod practice.

Having set up the mandala of the deity, you go on with the main part of the practice. The main part of the practice starts with the general Vajra Vehicle preliminaries then goes on to the offering that is specific to Chod practice. The first steps of the general Vajra Vehicle preliminaries are taking refuge and arousing enlightenment mind. To do that, first you have to have the object of refuge, so the text says,

> **PHAṬ** ꞉
> In the expanse of self-appearances, luminosity-great bliss, ꞉
> The space divorced from the elaborations of conceptual effort and activity, ꞉
> The root guru, the sixth one Vajradhara, ꞉
> The mind, symbol, and aural lineage gurus, yidam deities, ꞉
> Dakinis, dharmapalas, and guards massed like clouds, ꞉
> Are visible, unstopped, in the midst of a sphere of rainbow light. ꞉

This follows on from the immediately preceding instructions. There is the expanse of directly-experienced emptiness which has appearances in it. The appearance is connected with the expanse's luminosity. When there is a direct experience of the emptiness-luminosity, the appearances occurring within it are experienced as great bliss. A practitioner who can do this lives in a space in which all of this happens. Living in such a space, the practitioner has total knowledge without any of the elaborations—concepts—that would be present in a practice occurring in a space based on the dualistic ignorance of self-grasping.

Within that space, the root guru and all of the other three roots appear. The root guru is equated with Vajradhara who is the leader of all the five buddhas who lead the five families, therefore, he is called the sixth buddha. Note that this does not mean that he is lord of the six families but is the sixth buddha, lord over the five families.

Then there are the gurus of the three lineages by which the Nyingthig teaching is transmitted. The three lineages are: the mind lineage of the conquerors; the sign lineage of the vidyadharas; and the aurally heard lineage of ordinary persons. The first entails mind to mind contact between conquerors or buddhas. The second entails transmission via symbols and only happens at a very advanced spiritual level. The third is simply called "aural lineage" because it entails the very mundane approach of verbal transmission between ordinary beings or persons. The third is not a "hearing lineage" for "hearing lineage" is the name for a very special transmission of teachings which occurs privately and with many seals of secrecy. The third is also not an oral but "aural" lineage.

The guards are the various lesser dharma protectors.

All of the refuge objects are visible in a way which is un-stopped. Unstopped here does not mean that you are there undistractedly with the visualization, though that is desirable. This usage of unstopped is usually translated as a general term using "unhindered", "unceasing", and the like but it is not a term of general meaning. It is a special technical term that describes a specific quality which results when expanse and luminosity are in union together. This quality involves a very profound understanding of luminosity which is difficult to explain. See "not stopped" in the glossary for more.

Then it gives advice on how to do this refuge. This is not saying that the refuge is being done principally led by the demons, but that you are helping all beings to take refuge while paying special attention to helping the gods and demons. What is happening here is that you are helping them to take refuge by acting as the spokesman for all of them. Moreover, you are helping them to take a fully-informed, as opposed to blind-faith type or stupid, type of refuge.

With that, visualize the accumulation field and ꞉
Think that you lead all sentient beings, with gods and demons ꞉
Put foremost, in taking fully-informed refuge. ꞉

Then there is the verse for taking refuge:

> PHAṬ ༔
> Because of not knowing that this uncontrived, ༔
> Self-arising rigpa is the entity of the objects of refuge, ༔
> Beings are drowning in the ocean of suffering— ༔
> Please give them refuge with your mind of the three kayas. ༔

"Not knowing" is a literal translation of what is usually translated as "ignorance" but which is actually "not being in rigpa". Because sentient beings are in a state of not-rigpa, they do not know the actual fact of the Three Jewels and Three Roots, the objects of refuge. What is that fact? It is the very rigpa that you have firmly planted yourself in by doing the practice so far. It is called "self-arising rigpa" here because "self-arising" emphasizes that the rigpa is self-arising or self-existing, beyond the karmically-driven process of samsaric knowing. It is exactly because sentient beings have this not knowing, this not being in rigpa that they are drowning in the ocean of suffering of samsara. Now, you as the deity are supplicating on their behalf. You are saying, "Please you invited objects of refuge, give them refuge with your enlightened mind, which in its fullness is the mind of dharmakaya and the two form kayas that appear from it to benefit sentient beings."

Then the text says,

> *Repeat that three times then arouse the mind:* ༔

You repeat the refuge verse three times then you "arouse the mind" which is the standard term for arousing enlightenment mind. Enlightenment mind is aroused with the next verse:

> PHAṬ ༔
> The mind that grasps at appearances as things ༔
> Is totally severed by the conduct of yogic activity ༔
> Then in order to realize the actuality of reality ༔
> I arouse the mind freed from hope and fear. ༔

The dualistic, samsaric mind does not see appearances as they actually are but as "things"[30] where thing means a conceptually invented thing. This mind is totally severed—again the meaning of Chod—using the conduct of yogic activity that is the special feature of Chod. With that done, it is possible to arouse ultimate or superfactual enlightenment mind.

The text says that the reason for arousing this enlightenment mind is to realize the actuality of reality. "Reality" here is a translation of a Sanskrit term "bhuta" that the Tibetans translated as "the authentic". It is a noun meaning reality. What the practitioner needs to do is "to realize the actuality of reality", meaning to realize the actual situation of fundamental reality.

There are two types of enlightenment mind: fictional and superfactual[31]. When the two are unified, you have what is called "ultimate enlightenment mind" in which all appearances of the fictional are present but there is no grasping at them. That ultimate enlightenment mind is what you are arousing here. It has the characteristic of being capable of working for sentient beings but without any of the hope and fear that comes from dualistic grasping and which would distort the activities done for the benefit of others.

Next is the mandala offering:

> *Repeat that three times. Then offer a mandala, thinking that your torso is Mt. Meru, your limbs the four continents, your fingers and toes the sub-continents, your head the god abodes,*

---

[30] Tib. dngos po.

[31] The terms translated as "fictional" and "superfactual" here have been translated as "relative" and "absolute" for many years. However, there is almost no relationship between the meanings of "relative" and "absolute" and the original terms. See the glossary for more information.

your two eyes the sun and moon, and your inner organs the wealth of gods and men: ꞉

PHAṬ ꞉
Self-cherishing's aggregate, this illusory body, ꞉
Is fully arranged as the heaps of a mandala ꞉
Then offered without expectation to the deities of the
accumulation field. ꞉
May the root of self-grasping be cut! ꞉
PHAṬ ꞉

Self-cherishing is one aspect of grasping at a self. Your body is the aggregate produced by self-cherishing and also the aggregate looked after so closely all the time by self-cherishing. "Fully arranged" means that the whole thing is set out as a mandala. "Offered without expectation" means that it is given without idea of something coming back in return. The "deities of the accumulation field" are all the beings who were invited for taking refuge and who are still there. Deities in this case has the sense of "divinities". It is the "accumulation field" because it is the object through which merit and wisdom, the two accumulations, are gathered.

Next is the guru yoga,

PHAṬ ꞉
In the expanse without outflows, dharmakaya's space, ꞉
Amidst its lustre, a sphere of intermeshing rainbow rays, ꞉
Is the father, knower of all the three times,
Padmasambhava, ꞉
In the manner of a heruka whose conduct is yogic
activity, ꞉
Together with an ocean of mother dakinis assembled. ꞉

The expanse of emptiness that belongs to the state of wisdom is the space of dharmakaya. This space, because it is fruition realization, does not have any of the outflows that occur when wisdom loses itself and leaks out into dualistic mind. Dharmakaya is not only the space of the expanse; it also has output[32], as it is called. The output of wisdom turns into sensory appearances. "Lustre" here indicates the subtle output, like lustre, that is coming from the empty expanse of the dharmakaya. It is turning into the appearance of Padmasambhava. He appears in the midst of a sphere of light made of intermeshing rainbow-coloured light rays. The wording here does not mean "scintillating" but "intermeshing". The point is that the mass of light rays of five colours builds up into a massive sphere of light, with light rays swirling and whirling and intermeshing.

Padmasambhava's appearance here is specifically that of a heruka and his style is that of a heruka doing the yogic activity of Chod practice. He is the male and like the father for the practitioner. "Mother dakinis" refers to the wisdom dakinis who surround him. They are the female aspect and are like the mother for the practitioner.

Then the text says,

> Your body with the sparkling marks and signs is a lamp
> alight, alight. ꞉
> Your speech with dharma for those to be tamed is
> sounding, resounding. ꞉
> Your mind the state of luminosity, is the vajra essence. ꞉
> Your son supplicates you with intense devotion. ꞉

The ends of the first two lines are not mistaken; they reflect poetry contained in the Tibetan text. Reciting "a lamp, alight, alight" is meant to conjure up a sense of the actual brilliance of Padmasambhava's body lit up with the major and minor marks of enlightenment. Reciting "sounding, resounding" is meant to conjure up a sense of his speech, which comes forth as the sound of dharma for those who could be tamed by his teaching. The third line says that his mind is luminosity; this is the luminosity meaning wisdom

---

[32] See the glossary.

luminosity that comes when the unsurpassed Great Completion teachings have been practised to their fruition. Remember that unsurpassed Nyingthig Great Completion lays great emphasis on "the nature" aspect of the essence of mind, which is luminosity that is the vajra essence or sugatagarbha of all beings.

The Tibetan wording of the line which says, "Your son supplicates you with intense devotion", is somewhat ambiguous and could also be understood as, "Your daughter supplicates you with strong respect". That could make sense given that the person making the supplication is visualized as the wisdom dakini, but both oral instruction and commentaries are in agreement that the meaning here is the former, for example, the *Store of the Dakini's Secret, An Excellent Vase of Amṛita*[33] shows the meaning by expanding the words of the line to, "This son of yours who is tormented unceasingly with sufferings of various kinds supplicates you with the longing of intense devotion ..."

I would like to make it clear that removing the possibility of the female understanding here is not a matter of chauvinism; there is an ambiguity in the Tibetan text which allows the words concerned to be taken in either of the two ways mentioned above, but the instructions of the lineage show clearly which way it should be. Nonetheless, there is no reason why someone reciting the text could not change the word "son" to "daughter" when reciting the liturgy. Doing say could satisfy the needs of some and at the same time retain the fundamental meaning of the verse.

The text continues with a supplication for blessings so that the practice of Chod could be successfully completed. The name Cutter

---

[33] This is a very clear commentary to Jigmey Lingpa's text written by a disciple of Tshogdrug Rangdrol that very nicely clarifies the meaning of the text.

of Mara is another name for Chod; as explained earlier, the practice of Chod is a practice that cuts the maras.

It is common in Great Completion to talk about the fruition of the practice as "seizing the conqueror's level". This fruition happens when the dharmakaya is fully realized through the profound methods of Great Completion. At the end of the supplication you merge with the guru and enter equipoise on non-duality. The text says:

> Outwardly, the gods and demons' form is discursive thought risen up as an enemy; ༔
> Inwardly, hope and fear is the mind grasping at duality; ༔
> In between, various appearances are all the unfavourable conditions— ༔
> May the profound dharma, Cutter of Mara, ༔
> Cut them off right now, on this very seat! ༔
> So that the conqueror's level, expanse dharmakaya be seized, ༔
> Father, revered guru, please grant your blessings!
> PHAṬ PHAṬ PHAṬ ༔
>
> *Say that and dissolve the accumulation field into yourself.* ༔
> *Enter into equipoise of the non-dual state.* ༔

Note that the note tells you to dissolve the field of refuge into yourself[34]. After that you enter the equipoise of the non-dual state. Equipoise means an utterly one-pointed state.

Next is the section in which one's normal way of knowing in which the knowing is mixed with externalized, material things is changed to the enlightened way of knowing in which the knowing is mixed with the empty expanse of dharmakaya.

[34] The verb "to dissolve" here is a transitive form of the verb, not an intransitive one. Thus the text here does not say what the reader might be expecting that "the field of refuge dissolves into you".

The first part of this section brings out your pure portion. There can be impurities in pure water and when the impurity or the impure portion is removed, just the pure portion—water itself—is left behind. Similarly, your body produced from ignorance and the ripening of karmic latencies[35] is an impurity that has been produced right on top of your pure portion, rigpa. That impure portion is now released and the pure portion brought forth as the Wrathful Woman[36]. The text says,

> PHAṬ ༔
> Then this impure portion, the body of latencies, ༔
> Gross due to being very well fed and fattened, ༔
> Has the pure portion, rigpa brought out from within ༔
> In the form of the Wrathful Woman, with the sound of PHAṬ! ༔

Note that the first two lines create the image of the impure portion, this bloated body of ours. The commentary *Store of the Dakini's Secret, An Excellent Vase of Amṛita* clearly says that the meaning of the words here is that our body "is very corpulent because of the extreme attention we pay to feeding and fattening it", not that the body is "greasy".

The text continues,

> Having one face, two arms, flaying knife and skull cup, ༔
> She slices the skull off my body. ༔
> Spanning the thousandfold realm ༔

"Thousandfold realm" abbreviates "third-order thousandfold world system" which is a certain level of cosmos described by the Buddha. A third-order thousandfold world system consists of a thousand sets of Mt. Meru world systems taken as a first order system, then one

---

[35] See the glossary.

[36] Tib. khros ma. Throma.

thousand of those as a second order system, then one thousand of those as a third order system. In other words, it is a universe made of one thousand to the power three of world systems like our Mt. Meru-based world system. In the Buddhist system, there are uncountable numbers of such universes. To understand the point here you could think of a third-order thousandfold world system as the equivalent of our universe. You will see this type of world system mentioned in various ways a number of times after this in the text. The skull cup is as vast as that and sits on a tripod of hearth stones which are themselves complete skulls. The text says:

> It is placed on a hearth of three skulls and inside ꞉
> The body of elements set out as the feast is made ꞉
> By the light of the three syllables to blaze into amṛita. ꞉
> OṂ ĀḤ HŪṂ and HA HOḤ HRĪḤ ꞉

The "body of elements" is this body made up of the four elements earth, water, fire, and air. It is placed in a skull cup made from the skull cut from your own impure body and used to create the feast substance. "Made to blaze" is the standard metaphor used in this type of visualization for when the impure substance is turned into amṛita; it is used because the amṛita arises and blazes with light. The "and" in "OṂ ĀḤ HŪṂ and HA HOḤ HRĪḤ" is actually part of the verse; the Tibetan verse needs seven syllables and that is obtained for this line by adding the "and" between the two sets of syllables. However, when doing the practice, you leave out the "and". Then there is the instruction,

> *The more you recite them, the more it is purified, increased, and transformed.* ꞉

This does not give the instruction to recite the two sets of syllables OṂ ĀḤ HŪṂ and HA HOḤ HRĪḤ as many times as possible, but encourages you to work at the practice by pointing out that, the more of them you recite, the more that the feast substance will be purified, increased, and transformed.

The commentary *Store of the Dakini's Secret, An Excellent Vase of Amṛita* states that OṂ purifies away the impure things of bad and faulty actions connected with the offering substance in the skull, that ĀḤ washes away remaining impurities and increases the amount of the substance, and that HŪṂ transforms the substance into the five amritas, corresponding to the five wisdoms. The commentary states that HA brings a general state of joy to the amṛita, that HOḤ makes it pervaded by the taste of the joy of non-dual bliss-emptiness, and that HRĪḤ gives it the potency of being the five kayas and the five wisdoms having the ability to manifest in any whichever way. needed.

Then the distributions of the body are made. "Distribution" is a particular term that is used to refer to the handing out of something which is being put on offer. Here, three distributions are set out in all: multicoloured[37], red, and black.

First is the multicoloured distribution. The material body having been transformed into wisdom substance is distributed as a variety of nice things.

> *For the multicoloured distribution, that is developed* ꞉
> *Further into all things which are desirable to mind—* ꞉
> *Productive forests, food, clothing, medicine, and so forth.* ꞉

The first two lines more fully stated mean, "For the multicoloured distribution, you start with the amṛita just created and develop it further, increasing it into all the different things that mind would desire".

The Tibetan wording of the third line can easily be mistaken. It has the phrase "skyed tshal" which, because it is not part of the common

---

[37] This has been translated by some as "striped", but that is a mistake that comes because the black and white striped ropes of Tibet are, correctly, called multi-coloured.

Tibetan dharma vocabulary, has sometimes been altered by Tibetan editors. The phrase looks like the common Tibetan phrases "skyid tshal" meaning a grove created for relaxation and enjoyment and "skyed tshul" meaning "the way to create" so editors have sometimes altered the original wording of "skyed tshal" to ones of those two possibilities. The original term refers to groves of vegetation in which medicinal plants of all varieties grow causing medicinal substances to be produced. The medicines produced are then part of the multicoloured distribution.

The red distribution comes next with,

> *For the red distribution, the Black Wrathful Woman,* ꞉
> *Flays the skin from your own impure-portion body,* ꞉
> *Spreads it out to span the third-order thousandfold world,* ꞉
> *Piles bodies, flesh, and blood into a heap on top,* ꞉
> *And you think of it as a slaughterhouse.* ꞉

Note that it does say "impure-portion" body and not just gross body or something similar. This specifically relates back to the impure-portion body explained earlier. This same wording is also used further on with the same meaning. The third-order thousandfold world system was described above. When the English text says "slaughterhouse" above, the Tibetan literally says, "a place where butchers like to do their work".

The black distribution comes next with,

> *For the black distribution, think that all diseases and dons,* ꞉
> *Evil deeds and obscurations, accumulated beginninglessly* ꞉
> *By sentient beings, yourself and others, condense into* ꞉
> *A black cloud that dissolves into the heap of bodies* ꞉
> *And the gods and demons devour it, making their* ꞉
> *Bodies turn black like charcoal.* ꞉

The feast section follows the distributions. Generally speaking, a Vajra Vehicle feast is done in two parts: an offering first for the higher beings followed by one for the lower beings. There is a point of terminology that the first offering is specifically called "offering" which translates "puja" and the second is specifically called "giving" or "being generous". In Chod, the first part is the standard offering made to the three roots, and so on, whereas the second part is done using the yogic activity of offering one's body.

To start a feast, the guests must be summoned. Thus the text says,

> *Call out to the guests of the offering and generosity like this:* ꞉
>
> PHAṬ ꞉
> You the recipients of offering, the three roots and
> samaya'd ones, ꞉
> Then you the recipients of generosity, principally of the
> eight classes of elementals, ꞉
> Up through the demons and dons of retribution, ꞉
> Come to this place of yogic activity's conduct! ꞉

The Tibetan says, "Starting with the recipients of offering", which is the higher beings. The higher beings are the three roots and the ones who have samaya because of having been bound by oath to protect the dharma.

Then the text says, "And going on to the recipients of generosity", which is the lower beings. For Chod practice, the lower beings are all lower beings but with emphasis placed on the eight classes of elementals. Elementals could be called spirits. The Tibetan term literally says "elementals" and corresponds exactly to the term "elementals" used in Europe when gods and demons were still part of that culture. The eight classes of elementals is a summary of many different types of elementals under eight heads; it was brought from Indian culture into Tibet and the full list is explained in detail in the *Illuminator Tibetan English Dictionary*[38].

And then, specifically, out of all of them, there are the demons and dons with whom the practitioner has actual karmic debts that will result in karmic retribution.

The sense of the text overall here is "starting with the higher beings, and then going on through the lower beings all the way through to the most prominent ones in this practice", the most prominent ones being the ones with whom the practitioner has serious karmic debts.

Generally speaking, if a being has done something which has adversely affected another sentient being, then the first being has a karmic debt with the second one. If the action was such that the being who has been harmed could try to retaliate in the future because of karma, then the first being has created what is called a debt of retribution. If the retaliation does happen, there is no longer a debt but a retribution that has taken place. There are many types of retribution mentioned in the Chod system.

Now the practitioner sets up the special Chod feast of his own body:

> Today, I the fearless yogin ꞉
> Arrange this illusory body that parts samsara and nirvana ꞉
> In a kapala having the area of a third order world ꞉
> As the feast offering of the grand lifeless corpse. ꞉
> I transform it into amrita of un-outflowed wisdom. ꞉
> This magical display that appears as the various desires ꞉
> Offered without the grasping of self-cherishing ꞉
> Is a grand feast indeed, please come as the guests! ꞉
> Oh the sound of the great supreme skull drum so bright! ꞉

[38] By Tony Duff, first published in 2001 by Padma Karpo Translation Committee.

Oh the melody of the great grounds' trumpet so sweet! ȿ
Oh the flash of the bells, little bells, and chevrons so delightful! ȿ
Just like vultures flocking to flesh, ȿ
Please come here, this instant! ȿ
PHAṬ ȿ

"Illusory body which parts samsara and nirvana" means this body of mine, which is an illusory thing, and which is being used here in order to do the Great Completion practice called "Parting Samsara and Nirvana into their Respective Sides", usually abbreviated to "ru shan" in Tibetan.

"Third order world" is another abbreviation of third-order thousandfold world, which was explained previously. The "grand" lifeless corpse is a human lifeless corpse; "grand" here is another code word for human items. "Un-outflowed wisdom" as explained before is wisdom that is not becoming confused and leaking out of its self-contained state into dualistic ignorance and all that goes with it. "As the various desires" means the wishes of or what is desired by all of the different sentient beings. The Tibetan text actually mentions nine types of sentient being in this phrase because of calculating that there are three types of being in each of the three realms and each has their own set of wishes. The amṛita is seen to be something that fulfills the wishes of every possible sentient being, which it is because it is wisdom based. The words "great supreme" and "great grounds" are more code words for "human". The sound of the skull drum in the Tibetan is literally "crisp and clear" but somehow "bright" seems a more fitting translation in English. The description of the bells, little bells, and chevrons is literally that they are "delightful because of being so pure", but it means that their movements, and sounds, and so on are brilliant little flashes in the overall scene.

The one really major difference between the various editions of this text that we consulted is found here. The Shechen Monastery edition and many others have the words,

> Oh the melody of the great grounds' trumpet so
> sweet! ꞉

People who use this edition maintain that it is correct. However, there is another edition that inserts several words so that the line above becomes two lines as follows:

> Oh the splendour of the hide of a human with the great
> grounds! ꞉
> Oh the melody of the human thighbone trumpet so
> sweet! ꞉

People who follow that edition, for example those at Dzogchen Monastery, maintain that it is correct. A human with the great grounds is a person who has made ten specific transgressions that qualify him to be killed by a vajra master.

Then there is offering to the higher beings and dedication. Offering, as mentioned above, is not the same as the giving done for the lower beings.

Then there is the offering and dedication: ꞉

PHAṬ ꞉
To the vidyadhara gurus of the Three Lineages ꞉
Starting with the primordial protector ꞉
And going through to the root guru, ꞉
And to the yidams, dakinis, and dharma protectors, ꞉
I make the offering of the amṛita of the grand lifeless
corpse. ꞉
May I and others, with gods and demons brought to the
fore, ꞉
Complete the two accumulations and purify the two
obscurations. ꞉

Due to taking yogic activity to its end for the benefit of
migrators, ꞉
May appearances be trained into luminosity-illusion and ꞉
Dread and anxiety be liberated into dharmakaya. ꞉
Please bless me to be heruka in style. ꞉

The three lineages are as described earlier. The primordial protector is the most primordial principle, the place where the whole lineage of teaching starts, which is Samantabhadra. "Grand" again means human. In general in Great Completion there is a twofold need to train appearances into unification through the path of discovering them to be the illusions of luminosity and to liberate all of the content of dualistic mind into dharmakaya. The lines end with a request to be a heruka kind of person, because this is the practice of Chod. It does not say "like a heruka" but a "heruka kind of person", and specifically, as mentioned before, a heruka who has the Chod style of conduct.

"Migrators" is a very commonly-used word for sentient beings. The term in Sanskrit and Tibetan literally means "goers". The term gives the specific sense of beings who are in a constant state of migration as they go from one existence to another. The example given when this word is explained is that beings in samsara are like flies buzzing around in a jar, zooming from one place to another and resting for a moment before zooming off again. Avoiding the actual meaning of the term and replacing it with "beings" loses the image that is being presented of the condition of sentient beings.

Then there is the generosity done for the lower beings:

PHAṬ ꞉
To the eight classes of elementals, to the non-humans ꞉
Who have transcended this world and who have not, ꞉
And to the host of flesh-eating dons who lead beings
astray, ꞉
I offer on top of a human hide spanning the third-order ꞉

Thousandfold world heaps of flesh, blood, and bones. ꞉
If I grasp at a self, oh how weak I am! ꞉
If you cannot do it, you are even worse! ꞉
If you want it now, swallow the raw flesh whole! ꞉
If you have no hurry, cook it in chunks and eat it! ꞉
Don't leave behind even a speck! ꞉

Note that it is not a "tarpaulin" or other such possibilities that is used to cover the third order thousandfold world. Rather, it is a human hide; the word used in the text is another code word for human parts. Note the last line; the Tibetan term translated here as "speck" actually means "a very small bit". It could be translated as "atom" but in this context it means a speck or a crumb.

Then a dedication is made for the lower beings:

PHAṬ ꞉
For those who from beginningless time in samsara ꞉
Have retributions resulting from murderous grudges, ꞉
And those who just came by for the leftovers, guests of my compassion, ꞉
And every one of those who is menial and has no say, ꞉
I dedicate an inexhaustible treasure of desirable objects ꞉
Of the senses, according to whatever you individually want! ꞉
May all connected to me, both good and bad, become buddhas and ꞉
Be cleansed of their debts of retribution. ꞉
PHAṬ ꞉

The first two lines say, "In particular and counting through the whole time without beginning of samsara, all those beings with whom I have karmic debts that come from me having harmed them and their having borne murderous or other seriously harmful grudges towards me that will result in retribution are specifically invited". Then the third line includes all the rest of the lower beings who might not be the special objects of compassion of the Chod practitioner but who are the objects in general of the practitioner's compassion. These are the lower beings who have, the text literally says, just dropped in for the occasion, given that they have seen that there is a handout and they can get it. In other words, the first is a specific type of lower being guest for this Chod practice and the second is the rest of the lower being guests in general. Then, within all the beings of those two types who have arrived for the handout, there will be those who will have trouble getting any of the handout because of being the most menial; the fourth line specifically ensures that they too will be able to get whatever they want.

"May all be connected to me both good and bad become buddhas and …" is the shortest way I could find to say what in Tibetan is only three words but which in English comes out to "may the whole extent of those who have positive and obstructive relationships with me become buddhas". The next line means that, of them, may any who have karmic debts of any sort that would result in retribution be cleansed of those karmic debts.

Then the text says,

> *Saying that, give without reservation.* ꞉

which is similar to "give without expectation of return" and has the same meaning.

Then comes the phase of dissolving the practice back into emptiness:

> *Enter into equipoise on the state of emptiness.* ꞉

Following that is advice on how to rouse the assurance needed to deal with fears that might arise during the giving.

> *At that point, if you have self-cherishing for body* ꞉
> *And fearful hesitation appears in mind,* ꞉

Rouse assurance with the thought, ࿑
"The body, having been given to the gods and demons, is gone ࿑
And mind is free of ground and root— ࿑
Let alone the demons, even the buddhas do not see it", and ࿑
Decide firmly that what comes up in mind is your own face. ࿑

Essentially, the body has already been given away so there is no point in worrying yourself about that and the mind cannot be found as a solid thing, so there is nothing about you at all that could really be harmed. Therefore, "decide firmly", meaning that you should make a firm decision and stay with that decision henceforth, that whatever comes into your mind is in fact you seeing the very entity of your own mind, and not anything other than that.

Then comes advice on the sorts of harmful appearance that might occur. The text says that there are four types of maras which can be encountered in this practice and that any that are encountered should be cut using the experience of the space-like expanse of emptiness. Note that the first two lines have annotations in the Tibetan text which are not part of the original revealed treasure. They are the equivalent of English text in parentheses so are shown as such.

There are maras that have physical substance (note in text: outer conditions such as the elements, wild beasts, violent men, and so on, and the discursive thoughts of attachment, anger, and so on) and maras that do not (note in text: internal conditions such as mind's moods of happiness and sadness, and so on) ࿑
Maras of outer enjoyments (note in text: thinking only of yourself; the conceit of being concerned with one's own happiness, and so on) and maras of holier than though attitudes (note in text: doubt, hesitation, and so on). ࿑
Exclaim PHAṬ and sever them in the expanse!

The next lines indicate the timings and reasons for doing the distributions that are special to Chod:

> *In the early dawn period, in order to complete the two accumulations* ꞉
> *The white distribution is done to increase the amṛita substance;* ꞉
> *At mid-day, in order to purify retributions* ꞉
> *Dedicate the multicoloured distribution where suitable;* ꞉
> *In the evening, in order to rouse the path of yogic activity* ꞉
> *Perform the red distribution to totally sever grasping at a self;* ꞉
> *In the early night, to purify evil deeds do the black distribution.* ꞉

Then the text gives general advice on how to do them,

> *All of these involve transformation of your outlook,* ꞉
> *So the main thing is to practise by doing the visualization.* ꞉

"Transformation of outlook" means a change in how you look at yourself and where you focus your drive because of it. Therefore, the underpinning of all these practices is to visualize yourself as the wisdom dakini, for that eliminates the concept of yourself as your ordinary self and transforms it into a concept of yourself as an enlightened kind of person, providing a suitable basis for all the different distributions.

Then the general advice is given that, no matter what trickery of illusion appears the appearance must be adjusted using the view. That can be done because all appearance is a fiction. However, do not do it with a view connected with temporary experience, meaning a view that is only partially complete. As was discussed at the very beginning of the text, appearance must be adjusted with pure view, meaning a view without any conceptual sidetracks in it.

> *At that time, no matter what trickery of illusion occurs,* ꞉
> *Adjust it with the view freed of temporary experience.* ꞉

It might be that your view is not very full or pure. In other words, you might not be very good at bringing rigpa to the appearance. If that is the case, the amount of empty expanse that you have available in your yoga or practice to mix with the storm provoked could be too small for you to successfully adjust the appearances that occur.

"What is provoked" is a term in Tibetan that literally means an upheaval. It is only used for unexpected upheavals of mind which have the potential to scare you or worse. The question is, can you deal with them or not? If you can, then it is said that they are "finished with". Upheavals are finished with by taking charge of them and mixing them with empty expanse. Then they cease to be fear inducing and the karmic seeds that cause them are "finished with" or done with. Thus there are these two terms of provocation and "finishing with" in Chod practice.

If you as the practitioner do not have or cannot bring enough empty expanse to your mind, then the practice will not be successful and it could become dangerous. Alternatively, the gods and demons could be more expansive in their minds than you in which case you would not be able to cause any provocation and the practice would not work. If that is the situation, you should do the enhancing practice of the white skeleton:

> *If the degree of expanse with the yoga is small and* ꞉
> *The storm of what is provoked is difficult to adjust or* ꞉
> *The gods and demons, having a greater expanse, are not provoked,* ꞉
> *You should do the visualization of the white skeleton.* ꞉

This is the point in the text where the enhancement practice of the system is explained. The text outlines the practice then mentions its special capability, which is that it is particularly effective at overcoming contagious diseases that can be fatal. The text says:

Saying "PHAṬ", instantly I become ꞉
A white skeleton, blazing with fire. ꞉
A fire arises from its enormous size that ꞉
Incinerates the thousandfold world and ꞉
Particularly the dwelling place of the gods and demons. ꞉
Finally, the skeleton together with the fire ꞉
Turns to light and vanishes, and you stay in the state of emptiness. ꞉
This practice is particularly effective at giving protection
against contagious disease. ꞉

The wording "enormous size" is indistinct in some editions of the Tibetan text. Because of that, the Tibetan text has sometimes been altered to a wording that looks similar to the original but which means "great heat". However, lineage gurus say that it is definitely "enormous size" as it appears in the text. That is so because of the instruction that the skeleton is to be visualized as enormous, the size of the whole universe.

The text continues with advice on what to do if you have not been able to successfully "finish with" what comes up and have managed to get yourself targeted by malevolent gods and demons.

If signs of finish in the practice do not arise in a timely way, ꞉
And malevolent demons target you for violence, ꞉
Make your rigpa evident in the form of the Wrathful Woman ꞉
And think that she flays the skin from your impure-portion body ꞉
And makes it into a human skin covering the three thousandfold world. ꞉
She lays a carpet of flesh and bones out on top of it ꞉
Which the demons and obstructors indeed long to devour. ꞉
At that moment, Wrathful Lady gathers up the human skin all at once, ꞉
Ties it with a lasso of snakes and intestines, ꞉
Whirls it overhead and smashes it down, ꞉

Making pulp of their flesh and bones. ༔
Many emanation wild beasts consume it, ༔
Leaving nothing. ༔

When you have done that,

Mix expanse and rigpa, and enter equipoise. ༔
Certainty of finish in the practice will arise and ༔
The violence of the demons and dons will have been eliminated; ༔
The rational mind that grasps everything with self-cherishing having been abandoned, ༔
Everything will be cherished by assurance of the view. ༔

Mixing expanse and rigpa is a key instruction of Nyingthig Great Completion. When you have equipoise on mixed expanse and rigpa, you will have a full and pure rigpa and will be able to carry the practice through to the point where you have the finishing aspect of dealing with whatever comes up. That in turn will mean that the gods and demons causing you trouble will have been eliminated, and so on.

The Vajra Vehicle has what are called the "certainties" of practice. They are specific states of realization that occur when the practice or some part of the practice is taken to its final point. An important certainty of Chod practice is that the practitioner actually can do "finishing" as mentioned above. All in all, it is possible to reduce Chod practice down to provoking upheavals then finishing with them.

There is a play on "cherishing" here. For as long as finishing does not happen in the practice, self-cherishing is uppermost. However, when this certainty of the practice has been obtained, cherishing the view—meaning that the practitioner is in the view all the time—becomes uppermost.

When the yogin can provoke and finish with upheavals, he continues on with the practice in order to get to the fruition. That causes him to move along the path. As he does so, there will be temporary experiences which indicate that the path is progressing. The text next sets out some of the possibilities of the temporary experiences of Chod practice and does so in relation the two things of provocation and finishing:

> At that time, signs of: provocation like finishing, ༔
> Finishing like provocation; ༔
> And also a mixture of both; ༔
> And latencies like both; ༔
> And finishing and provocation both finalized; ༔
> Will be the temporary experiences that come from doing the conduct. ༔

Temporary experiences will be sidetracks if clung to or taken as final. There can be signs of temporary experience where provocation looks like finishing and vice versa, there can be both mixed, there can be latencies coming out that look like both mixed, and there can be temporary experiences that seem to be the finalization of both. Ask your guru for more instructions on the details.

The text continues by showing the fruition that comes with the finalization of the practice. Temporary experiences are not signs of finalization. What are the signs of finalization? In this practice, it is when the practitioner can bring all of the practice into a lived space of emptiness:

> *It is when you have entered the space in actual fact ༔*
> *Of the mind of selflessness, Samantabhadri, ༔*
> *The great mother Prajnaparamita, ༔*
> *That the Cutter's Object will have come about as the path. ༔*
> ***SAMAYA ༔***

The lived space of emptiness is called Samantabhadri in Great Completion terminology and is called "the great mother of all the conquerors Prajnaparamita" in the general terminology of Chod practice. The text here is saying that it is not until that space is being lived that the Cutter's Object, meaning the maras, will have been dealt with through using them as path. When that has been achieved, the practice has been mastered.

Concluding Section

Now, the text says,

> *In conclusion, the prayers of dedication and aspiration:* ༔

First there is a verse of dedication which says that even though a practitioner has experienced liberation into dharmakaya's emptiness, the interdependency connected with his illusory activities still has to be dedicated and has to be dedicated within the state of non-dual wisdom. This is what is called superfactual or ultimate dedication.

> AḤ
> When the mass of concepts, virtuous and unvirtuous, is self-liberated, ༔
> The concept labels[39] of hope and fear are not referenced ༔
> But the infallible interdependency of the appearing factor, the continuity of the mass of virtue, ༔
> Has to be dedicated within the un-outflowed dharmadhatu. ༔

That dedication is followed by a prayer of aspiration specifically for Chod practice:

> PHAṬ ༔
> Through the generosity of the fictional body, ༔
> May those with debts of retribution accumulated over kalpas have them purified and ༔

[39] See the glossary.

When their mindstreams have been liberated by the truth
of superfactual dharma, ༔
May they appear as the first ones in my assembly. ༔
At that time, when the uncontrived, self-present, innate
fact ༔
Has been produced in the mindstreams of the unruly gods
and demons, ༔
Instead of following after the confusion of grasping at
"I", ༔
May their mindstreams be moistened with love and
compassion. ༔
And for myself, having taken the conduct of yogic activity
to completion, ༔
May happiness and sadness have their taste equalized with
samsara and nirvana trained into dharmakaya. ༔
May I be victorious in all directions with every connection
that I make a meaningful one, ༔
And may I take enlightened activity to completion and
accomplish a rainbow body! ༔
PHAṬ ༔

The next line,

Say that, while preserving the lustre in the state of the view. ༔

tells you that the way to make the dedication and aspiration is to remain in equipoise in the state of the view while maintaining the lustre of the empty aspect of the view. The words "preserving" and "lustre" are terminology of Great Completion and have profound instruction connected with them; see the glossary for more information. Essentially, this is pointing out how to live in unified emptiness and appearance while doing whatever you do. This advice applies to the last verses being recited but is also the first line of several lines of general advice on how to make one's whole life into practice. The lines continue with:

Placing importance on great compassion, ༔
Do the visualization of sending and taking (note in text: sending my own happiness to the gods and demons and taking the gods and demons suffering onto myself) happiness and suffering, ༔

In other words, preserving appearance as the lustre of the view is the basic practice of Great Completion. The other main practice that goes with that is the practice of fictional enlightenment mind, which is accomplished using the practice of sending happiness and taking suffering[40]. Chod also emphasizes generosity of dharma, which is one of the three types of generosity explained in the paramita of generosity. The final line, about making connections into the path of emancipation, uses the terminology of positive and negative connections mentioned earlier and is specifically about the practice of Chod.

The text continues,

And do totally pure generosity (note in text: that is, say these expressions of auspiciousness: "All dharmas arise from causes ..." and, "Do no evil deeds whatsoever ..." and "May those spirits left here still ...") of dharma. ༔

The note in the text that explains the meaning of performing generosity of dharma identifies three verses to be recited in order to perform generosity of dharma by mentioning the first line only of each one. Here is the note written out in full so that you have the three verses complete:

Say these expressions of auspiciousness,

All dharmas arise from causes.
Those causes were stated by the tathagata.

---

[40] Tib. gtong len.

What the cessation away from those causes is
Is what the great sage has spoken about.

and,

Do no evil deeds whatsoever and
Do engage in a perfection of virtue.
Thoroughly tame your own mind.
This is the teaching of Buddha.

and,

May those spirits left here still and
Any on the earth or then again in the sky,
Perpetually have loving kindness for the nine beings,
And carry out dharma day and night!

The first verse to be recited is the famous statement made by a junior monk of Shakyamuni Buddha when he met Shariputra who was on the way to meet the Buddha for the first time. Shariputra asked what the teaching of the Buddha was and this answer was given. It sums up the whole of the Buddha's dharma in a statement about interdependency. On hearing it, Shariputra became an arhat, so it is regarded as something that Buddhists should recite. It is called the heart of interdependency because it states interdependency as taught by Shakyamuni Buddha in its most essential form.

The verse following that is a very famous statement made by the Buddha himself that sums up the entirety of his teaching. There is a special way in the Great Completion tradition of commenting on the first three lines so the prayer is often used in the tradition.

The final verse is for the gods and demons, including any still present after the practice and all the others in general, both those on land and in the sky. The nine beings are, as mentioned before, a way of including all the beings throughout the three realms.

Then the text says,

> *Make positive relations and obstructive connections, good and bad, into the path of emancipation.* ༔

Which is a summary of the practice of Chod.

Then the text says:

> ***SAMAYA* ༔ *MA MA KO LING SAMANTA* ༔**

which shows the end of the revealed treasure.

There is an addition to the end of the text that is not part of the revealed treasure. It shows the musical annotation for blowing the thighbone trumpet. Five melodies are shown with a very brief description for each. The five correspond to the five chakras in general and the appropriate seed-syllable is shown for each.

Profound Foremost Instructions For the Chod Practice Sound Of Dakini Laughter by Dza Patrul

Great sword of Vajra Sharpness,
The supreme syllable, is the complete purity
Of the great vehicle that Cuts suffering;
I pay homage to the great weapon PHAṬ.

Paramita totally complete and
Totally decorated with all the levels
Is the dharma of complete purity, non-self;
I will write about the practice of profound meaning
Cut.[41]

---

[41] Dza Patrul's poetry here is very terse. Vajra Sharpness is the name of a particular form of Manjushri whose quality is vajra sharp prajna. The sword of this Manjushri is the vajra sharp sword of ultimate prajna. In the Chod system, this vajra sharp prajna is manifested specifically in the form of the syllable PHAṬ. In Chod it is called the supreme syllable because it is the consummate means in the system for cutting through to the complete purity of the non-self taught in the Great Vehicle. Chod is explained to be "that which cuts suffering" and it does that through the agency of this supreme syllable.

The Great Vehicle teaches a path of the paramitas. The ultimate attainment of the Great Vehicle occurs when the path of the paramitas has been totally completed. It is equivalent to the full realization of the
(continued ...)

When the instructions of that profound meaning are put into practice, there are, according to *The Chod Practice Sound of Dakini Laughter*, these to be done: preliminaries consisting of purifications; a main part consisting of practices that come down right on the central key points—introduction to the fact of the ground Mother[42], cutting the four maras into expanse, and so on; and a conclusion consisting of the enhancing conduct of bypassing[43] done at the time of going to terrifying places which is comprised of the visualizations

---

[41] (... continued)
Great Vehicle and as such is adorned with all the realizations developed on the journey through the ten levels of a bodhisatva. That full realization corresponds to the ultimate prajna mentioned in the first verse. It sees the complete purity of the absence of self taught in the Great Vehicle. He will now give some teaching on Chod, which is a practice of this profound meaning of the Great Vehicle.

[42] "Mother" throughout this text refers to "mother Prajnaparamita". The ground mother means the actual wisdom that exists in the ground of a practitioner's mind rather than a conception about it. The fact of the ground mother is what appears to the mind of the practitioner when the actual wisdom is met in direct perception. Introduction to this fact occurs either initially when it is introduced by the guru or following that when one's own innate wisdom introduces this fact to itself. See introduction in the glossary for more.

[43] Most systems of dharma have a main practice designed to bring forth the main meaning and one or more special enhancing practices designed to bring that main meaning out further so that it is more starkly experienced. The enhancers of Chod involve the practice of yogic disciplines so, out of view, meditation, and conduct, are placed in the category of conduct and are called enhancing conducts. Mahamudra and Great Completion differentiate two types of the conduct of view, meditation, and conduct: one which is engagement in a specific activity to achieve a specific goal; and one which bypasses all activities of conduct and simply returns to the view and meditation. The latter is called either "bypassing" or "conduct of bypassing".

for the three sets of subjugation[44] and the practice of casting aside the aggregate body.

1. The subjugating visualization done before leaving[45]

Think the following. The expression of PHAṬ causes a vajra to come from your heart centre. It is a nine-pointed, meteoric iron[46] vajra dense and unyielding, hefty and solid, emitting light rays and sparks from its ball of fire. You shoot it off towards the terrifying place like the arrow of a mighty archer. It goes there, descending like the meteoric iron of thunderbolts[47]. On arrival it emits lights and light rays and spits out sparks all over the place from its ball of fire. All of this makes the various types of gods and demons together with their hordes who are dwelling there powerless to run away and scatter and breaks their pride and will to fight. The gods and demons having lost their holier than thou attitudes, they remain there with a subdued manner.

Having done that and before you leave for that place, as it says in the text, "Rather than taking a condescending stance towards the gods

---

[44] In general, in Chod there are three sets of subjugations—those of self, place, and gods and demons. In terms of the practice, there are two distinct phases in which the subjugations are done—a phase done before leaving for the place of practice and a phase done after arrival at the place of practice. The two phases of subjugation include all three sets of subjugation.

[45] This whole section is what you have to do before you actually go to a terrifying place. You think to yourself that you do have to go to such a place. After that and before leaving, you first do the visualization then adjust your motivation for going.

[46] See the glossary for meteoric iron.

[47] The meteoric iron that accompanies thunderbolts rains down with an enormous force, smashing everything in its path. Again, see the glossary.

and demons or being driven by thoughts of the eight worldly concerns", you take up the assurance of the view of the realization of actuality—the absence of self—and the attitude of compassionate bodhicitta that thinks, "I will act for the sake of all the god and demon migrators that I meet, with the aim of setting them on the path of emancipation".

2. The subjugating visualization done while there[48]

Having arrived there, you do this visualization. With the exclamation of "PHAṬ", you visualize yourself, instantly, as the wisdom dakini of the secret[49], great-bliss Vajrayogini. With her mind of great compassion she has affection for sentient beings and has brought the three realms under her control; as signs of these, her body is red and blazes with light like of the fire of the end of time. Her mind is the lived space of great-bliss wisdom in which the three poisons have been purified into expanse and she has overwhelmed the three becomings[50] with her presence; as signs of these, she blazes with the brilliance of one hundred thousand suns and has a wrathful mood. Because her coarse and subtle mental latencies have been purified into the expanse and she has become sovereign over the mind inexhaustible wheel of ornamentation[51], her upper body is brilliant at the formless peak of existence; because her subtle latencies of self have been purified into the expanse and she has become sovereign over the speech inexhaustible wheel of ornamentation, the

---

[48] This is the subjugation as a whole that you do during your stay in the terrifying place.

[49] "Of the secret" means of the path of the secret, the Vajra Vehicle.

[50] See the glossary.

[51] "Inexhaustible wheel of ornamentation" is a phrase of the tantras. It is used to refer to the body, speech, and mind of someone who has become enlightened. It requires a lengthy explanation so will not be explained here.

waist region of her body is magnificent in the form realm; and because her coarse latencies of body have been purified into the expanse and she has become sovereign over the body inexhaustible wheel of ornamentation, the lower part of her body is on display in the abodes of the desire realm. Thus, with this dance of great bliss illusion, she manifests a vajra dance that fills the three becomings with her mudras[52]. Because samsara and nirvana are complete in the one universal sphere of the lived space of her unchanging dharmakaya, she has one face. As the sign that through knowledge she does not abide in becoming and has severed the confusion of the extreme of becoming, her lustrous black hair is bound up in a topknot. As the sign that through compassion she does not abide in the extreme of peace[53] and has stopped clinging to it, her long tresses of hair hang down, covering her back. Because her three kayas are spontaneously existing and she looks on migrators while exercising compassionate activity[54], she has three round and bloodshot eyes that are wide open. Because she performs works in this way for the aims of migrators through the four immeasurable ones and her four types of

---

[52] From the beginning down to here, there is a progression of ideas connected with the fact that she has brought all three realms of becoming, meaning samsara, under her control. Because of this she manifests throughout those three realms in various ways.

[53] The extreme of peace is the realization of an arhat in which one abides in personal peace without consideration of other sentient beings.

[54] Tib. thugs rje. "Compassionate activity" here does not mean compassionate activity in general but is a specific technical term for the dynamism of the spontaneous existence of enlightenment just mentioned. It is compassion-less compassion which perpetually acts for the welfare of all beings throughout the entirety of samsara and nirvana. Hence she has three eyes wide open and looking on at every aspect of all appearance and becoming.

activity[55] are uninterrupted, she bares her four sharp fangs with force. Because for her the branches of the melody of Brahma are complete[56] and confused appearance, the head of the dons, has been crushed, her tongue extends like red lightning and she exclaims the sounds of PHAṬ and PHEṂ. As the sign that, because method and prajna are unified beyond meeting and parting[57] she courses in the inseparability of samsara and nirvana via the vajra path, she has two arms. As the sign of her acting in great compassion and having completed the enlightened activity of the four ways of gathering,[58] her right hand waves a human hide of the ten grounds[59] red with a covering of blood with which she brings gods, demons, and humans all three under her control and makes them into her servants. As a sign of her being self-sounding dharma of prajna-emptiness that rouses the various types of beings from the sleep of ignorance, her left hand holds a human thighbone trumpet which she blows loudly, subjugating and defeating the worldly ones that make for

---

[55] These are the four types of activity of the tantras: pacifying, enriching, magnetizing, and destroying.

[56] Brahma has an exquisite voice with many aspects to its intonation. It is used in Buddhism as the example of what an enlightened person's voice is like. The meaning here is that she has perfected enlightened speech. Thus she is flicking her tongue at the maras, the representatives of fundamental confusion, and emitting the sounds that will overwhelm (PHAṬ) then magnetize them (PHEṂ).

[57] Beyond meeting and parting is a standard way to say that something has been fully realized. On the path, it will sometimes be experienced and sometimes not. At final realization, it will be changelessly present.

[58] The four ways of gathering disciples as explained in the Prajnaparamita teachings.

[59] A human hide of the ten grounds is the hide of a human who has created all ten grounds. The ten grounds are ten acts that make a person suitable to be killed by a Buddhist tantrika using the fourth karma, the activity of destroying.

haughtiness[60]. Having made the five poisons into the path and purified the five aggregates into the expanse, she enacts the aims of migrators through the five kayas and has completed the empowerments of the five families, therefore she has a crown of five dry skulls. As a sign that, on her body of the prajna mother consort, she has the five paramitas on the side of conduct, great method, she is adorned with the five symbolic ornaments made of bone. She sports in the expanse of the nine lived spaces because of having purified the latencies of the nine levels[61] and severed the enmeshing fetters, therefore she has the charms of the moods of the nine dances. Because she has the two accumulations united and has transcended the places of becoming and peace thus spontaneously accomplishes the two aims, her two feet move in dance[62].

---

[60] The worldly ones that make for haughtiness are those beings and states of mind that cause the haughtiness of samsaric attitudes. For example, like the haughty gods and demons.

[61] "Nine" refers to all samsaric possibilities of existence, three for each of desire, form, and formless realma. She has purified all of the latencies of all possible types of samsaric existence. Having done so, she has also severed the enmeshing fetters corresponding to all possible types of samsaric existence. Having done so, she appears in all of those existences but with them mixed with her realization of the expanse. Thus, for her they are lived spaces of realization rather than samsaric places. This is symbolized by the nine moods of a semi-wrathful deity, each of which has a corresponding dance. The nine moods of peaceful deities and the nine dances of wrathful deities are explained in detail in the *Illuminator Tibetan-English Dictionary*.

[62] She has the reached the ultimate possible realization in which the two accumulations of merit and wisdom are unified. This level of realization transcends both samsaric existence which is also called becoming and the arhats' existence which is also called peace. Because she has attained the realization of true complete enlightenment she spontaneously accomplishes both her own and others' aims. Her dancing with

(continued ...)

In space above her, all the lineage gurus of Chod move their bodies in the vajra dance, sound their speech in spontaneous songs sung in the melody of Brahma[63], and let their minds manifest in appearances of their mood of great bliss[64]. They sit within a mass of rainbows and lights, enveloped in majesty, full of light, and radiating warmth.

The space all around her is filled with the assemblies of deities of the yidams of the four and six tantra sections[65]. Their bodies are manifested in various ways within mountainous masses of fire and heaps of rainbows and light. Their speech resounds with the laughter of their delight. Their minds are the expression of great compassion. The peaceful ones are charming with their nine types of mood and the wrathful ones are on display with their nine types of dance.

In her retinue are the sacred charnel-ground protector dakinis: the group of one hundred thousand[66] body dakinis white, beautiful, and smiling; the group of one hundred thousand speech dakinis red and affectionate; the group of one hundred thousand mind dakinis blue and dancing; the group of one hundred thousand qualities dakinis

---

[62] (... continued)
two feet symbolizes her trampling on the incomplete realizations of samsara and arhats' lesser nirvana.

[63] Melody of Brahma is not a specific melody but means that their voices have the melody of Brahma which was explained in an earlier note. Essentially, it means that they sing in beautiful voices.

[64] A mind of realization knows emptiness and appearance unified. The unification leads to appearances appearing as great bliss. The gurus of the lineage have that realization and their minds have that mood.

[65] Each deity has its own assembly of deities.

[66] According to the oral instructions of the Longchen Nyingthig lineage, "group of hundred thousand" does not mean exactly one hundred thousand but that there are enormous numbers of them.

yellow and elegant; and the group of one hundred thousand activity dakinis green and fiercely wrathful. Amongst them, some show a youthful appearance with flowing tresses of glossy black hair and topknots, with bone ornaments, with bells and little bells jingling, and with various silken ribbons flying. Some show a more senior appearance; they are brilliant and awesome with yellow hair bound at the nape of the neck, are adorned with the fat and blood bindus[67] and wear old shrouds of a corpse, and go about their business cackling wild "ha ha's" with their toothless mouths and moving their bodies in dance. Some have a very peaceful and smiling appearance, some move about in the nine wrathful dances, and some have a mood half peaceful and wrathful. Having killed discursive thought in the expanse, some show the appearance of a murdering butcher. Having washed away the stains of latencies, some show the appearance of a cleaning washerwoman. Having transformed afflictions into wisdom, some show the appearance of a change-making dyer. Having been sustained by the experiences of samadhi, some show the appearance of a sustenance-providing cook. Having accepted all six classes of migrators, some show the appearance of a deceiving adulteress. On top of that, all of them because of living in the expanse of the view of empty rigpa are the dharmakaya expanse's full-fledged dakinis, and because of living in the expanse of meditation without grasping are present as sambhogakaya wisdom dakinis, and because of living in the expanse of conduct without clinging are manifest as nirmanakaya karma dakinis. And all of them having completed the fruition of being without attachment, all of the flesh-eating, worldly dakinis have been brought into their service.

Surrounding them are all the dharmapala guards—both those who act through wisdom and those who act karmically—whose manifestations of bodily colour and shape are not fixed and whose moods vary amongst the peaceful and wrathful moods. All of them also

---

[67] This is one specific decoration that comes from tantric symbolism.

have bodies exhibiting manifestations of dancing and stamping up and down, and speech that is broadcasting the song of HŪṂ and the sound of PHAṬ.

All of them like that—the principal deity together with her retinue—have minds which, with a mood of yogic activity style conduct, spread throughout samsara and nirvana inseparable and do the following for the purpose of overcoming the dualistic, discursive thoughts of samsara.

In the east, in the centre of a dance floor with a nature of great loving kindness, of transparent white rainbow light, and having the aspect of Purvavideha,[68] all angry thoughts, fierce wrath, are present in the form of the male don Gyalpo who is collapsed on the floor face down. By dancing up and down on him and the pacifying dance floor circular in shape, the anger is purified into mirror wisdom and the liveliness of the rigpa shines forth as the samadhi of great loving kindness. In the south, in the centre of a dance floor with a nature of great compassion, of transparent blue rainbow light, and having the aspect of Jambudvipa, all proud thoughts, haughtiness, are present in the form of the assembly of the killer Lord of Death's dons who are collapsed on the floor face down. By dancing up and down on them and the enriching dance floor square in shape, the pride is purified into the wisdom of equality and the liveliness of the rigpa shines forth in the form of great compassion. In the west, in the centre of a dance floor with a nature of great joy, of transparent red rainbow light, and having the aspect of Godaniya, all desire thoughts, clinging, are present in the form of the female don Rakshashi who is collapsed on the floor face up. By dancing up and down on her and the magnetizing dance floor semi-circular in shape,

[68] The name of the eastern continent of our Mt. Meru world system. In subsequent lines, the continent for each of the other three cardinal directions is mentioned and finally Mt. Meru is mentioned for the centre.

desire is purified into the wisdom of individual discrimination and the liveliness of the rigpa shines forth as the samadhi of great joy. In the north, in the centre of a dance floor with a nature of great equanimity, of transparent yellow rainbow light, and having the aspect of Uttarakuru, all jealous thoughts, malevolence, are present in the form of the cheating don Samaya-breaker who is collapsed on the floor face up. By dancing up and down on it and the destroying dance floor triangular in shape, jealousy is purified into the wisdom of all-accomplishment and the liveliness of the rigpa shines forth as the samadhi of great equanimity. In the centre, on top of a dance floor with a nature of enlightenment mind is a base of the four immeasurables with their four transparent lights surmounted by terraced steps of the four gatherings with brilliant colouration; it is the king of mountains Meru with its vast borders comprised of the six paramitas[69]. The appearances in their entirety that come from the confused thoughts which generate delusion, stupidity, are strewn all over that[70] as a carpet in the form of the gods and demons of appearance and becoming—the death demons, life demons, place demons who wander around, place dons, body dons[71], and so on. By dancing up and down on them and the magnificent dharmadhatu dance floor, delusion is purified into the wisdom of dharmadhatu and the liveliness of the rigpa by blazing up as enlightenment mind unifies emptiness and compassion. Then, samsara having been purified into nirvana, all the discursive thoughts of hope and fear,

---

[69] Mt. Meru is surrounded by rings of lesser mountains. Here they are the six paramitas.

[70] … Mt. Meru and environs just described in the previous sentence …

[71] These are the main ones. Death demons are ones that cause the problem of death such as by causing sickness. Life demons are ones that cause problems for the living. Place demons who wander around are demons who, inhabiting a certain place, wander around from there, causing trouble for other beings.

and acceptance and rejection, are purified into the expanse. Thinking that, perform the dance.

Think the following. Once again, light rays are emitted from your heart centre together with innumerable worker dakinis. They choicelessly hook the appearances which are confusion's form shining forth as dons, all the gods and demons of becoming, and especially, any malevolent gods and demons abiding in this area. With all of them collapsed on their backs, the dakinis plant stakes into their five limbs. Moreover, self-knowing dharmadhatu wisdom's self-output, meaning the output that it naturally produces without needing any causation for it, comes in the form of the vajra family dakini. She is white and has a peaceful, smiling, and beautiful mood. She plants white, round-shaped, peaceful stakes of her rigpa liveliness whose nature is great loving kindness into the right arm, whose nature is anger, of the gods and demons which are the form of self-grasping. By this, the thoughts of anger, harmful mind, now do not stir for even a moment and the samadhi of great loving kindness pops into clear view in the mindstream. Equality wisdom's self-output, the ratna family's dakini, yellow, and having a joyful and delighted mood, plants yellow, square-shaped stakes of her rigpa liveliness of great compassion into the left arm whose nature is pride. By doing so, the thoughts of pride, conceit, now do not stir for even a moment and the samadhi of great compassion is born in the mindstream. Self-knowing individually discriminating wisdom's self-output, the padma family's dakini, red and having a smiling and laughing mood, plants semi-circular-shaped magnetizing stakes of her nature of great joy into the left leg whose nature is desire. By doing so, the thoughts of desire, clinging, now do not stir for even a moment and the samadhi of great joy is born in the mindstream. Self-knowing all-accomplishing wisdom's self-output, the karma dakini, green and having a mood of fierce anger, plants black, triangular destroying stakes of her rigpa liveliness whose nature is great equanimity into the right leg whose nature is jealousy. By doing so, the thoughts of jealousy, competitive mind, now do not stir for even a moment and the samadhi of great equanimity is born in the mindstream. Self-knowing dharmadhatu wisdom's self-output, the buddha family's dakini, dark blue and having a mood that is a complete mood, one of joy of mixed wrath and passion, plants little stakes of her rigpa liveliness whose nature is aspiring enlightenment mind which are round circles, seal-knotted squares, bulging semi-circles, and pointy triangles[72]—that is, the four karmas spontaneously accomplished—into the head whose nature is delusion, ignorance. By doing so, body, speech, and mind all three are now not influenced by grasped-grasping for even a moment and abide together in the state of enlightenment mind. Thus the stakes are planted.

Having purified in that way all the appearances of the form of confusion—the gods and demons together with their dwelling places —into a lived space of the five wisdoms, think over and again the thought that, "The small tents in the expanse of complete purity which have the nature of the lived spaces of the five consorts, together with the dakini's palace, will remain for as long as samsara is not emptied"[73]. At the end of all that, you completely stop referencing your own presence and that of the gods and demons and, in the resulting state of empty rigpa free of elaborations,

---

[72] The adjectives for each of the four shapes such as "round" circle are the Tibetan ways of describing these four shapes, and mean no more than that. A seal-knotted square means that a square shape is a shape that is fully bounded.

[73] In other words, now that you have erected the enlightened realm of the dakini to start with and then totally immobilized all aspects of samsaric mind so that the enlightened realm cannot flow back into its samsaric aspect, you make the firm decision that this enlightened realm will henceforth remain as such. The enlightened realm consists of the lesser dwellings of the retinue dakinis and the palatial dwelling of the main dakini. The lesser dwellings are referred to as small tents because the small tent is the symbol of the view in Chod.

preserve the fact of the consort mother without wavering for even an instant from the practice of Prajnaparamita[74].

The three sets of subjugation—of self, abode, and gods and demons —are complete within these two phases of subjugation.[75] When the two phases are looked at in order to find their main points, the main points are found to be the subjugation of I and abode done by dancing up and down and the subjugation of gods and demons done by planting the stakes. Thus, the three sets of subjugation do not need to be sought elsewhere.

Upheavals of mind and paranormal events as explained in the instructional texts will occur because of doing these subjugating visualizations.[76] When that happens, it is time to undertake the actual practice of casting aside the body as food. This practice has three parts: preliminaries, main part, and conclusion.

1. Preliminaries

1. Taking Refuge

In the space before you, with you in your ordinary form, the root guru is present in the form of dharmakaya Great Vajradhara. He is surrounded by the lineage gurus of the conquerors' mind lineage,

---

[74] This is the equipoise referred to at this point in Jigmey Lingpa's text. It is described in Chod terminology as equipoise on the fact of ultimate Prajnaparamita.

[75] ... which have just now been described. Because these two phases of subjugation include all three sets of subjugation, the three sets of subjugation do not need to be sought elsewhere.

[76] Upheavals in the inner world of mind and strange events in the outer world which could be the doings of powerful ghosts and demons will be provoked by doing these subjugating visualizations.

the vidyadharas' sign lineage, and the peoples' aural lineage[77], together with the deity assemblies of the yidam mandalas, and the assembly of dakinis, dharmapalas, and guards. All of them together are like cloudbanks heaped up in the sky. Before them are you and your retinue of all sentient beings of the three classes with the three dons—place dons, body dons, and karmic dons—placed to the fore. All of you together are like crowds in a marketplace. Then you take refuge, thinking that you are doing so with body, speech, and mind rolled into one.

2. Arousing the Mind

Generally speaking, the aspiring mind, and so on should be understood as enumerated in the instructional texts[78] and roused in mind appropriately. Here, you specifically arouse the mind[79] with a thought like this, "Myself and others, all sentient beings, have from beginningless time clung to externally appearing objects as truly existent, solid things and have fallen under the control of establishing and negating, attachment and aversion.[80] I must totally sever

[77] These are the three lineages by which the Nyingthig teachings are transmitted. They are explained in the earlier commentary.

[78] Meaning the ones that are important to the system, such as Dza Patrul's *Words of My Perfect Teacher*, and so on. Aspiring mind is the aspiring enlightenment mind or aspiring bodhichitta. The Great Vehicle teachings enumerate many types of enlightenment mind. For example, aspiring, engaging, the twenty two types, and so on.

[79] Arouse the mind is the standard shorthand used in Great Vehicle texts and teachings for "arouse the enlightenment mind".

[80] "Establishing and negating, attachment and aversion" are examples of the sort of minds that operate when a being is living in dualistic mind; everything is always done in terms of dualities.

that using rigpa and the conduct of yogic discipline and so realize the actuality of reality[81]".

3. Mandala

In the systems of other texts, it is taught that awareness and matter are to be separated[82] and that, once the skin has been peeled away, the sequence of visualizations that goes with the words, "On the great golden ground ..."[83] is to be done.

However, in the system of this text[84], the practice here is not talked about in terms of separation of awareness and matter. Instead, the mind that conceives of the body as something very dear is turned into the agent of the offering and the limbs and related parts of the body which are conceived of as very dear are mentally designated as the four continents, Mount Meru, sun and moon, and so on. With that visualization, the practitioner divorces himself from the conception that this body is very dear then offers it to the deity assemblies

---

[81] "Actuality of reality" was explained in the previous commentary.

[82] "Systems of other texts" means the general system of Pacifier Chod as it is set out in various texts of that system with their various ways of explanation. In all of their explanations, there is an instruction here that "awareness and matter are to be separated". Awareness here simply means the knowing mind and matter means external objects known by that mind. The instruction means that the process of the practitioner's awareness has to be reversed so that it is no longer outwardly oriented and involved with solidified matter but is inwardly oriented and involved with just the awareness itself. It is a step towards realizing the nature of mind. This instruction includes the phrase, "skin being peeled away" which means again that the husk of believing in materiality is being removed, leaving just the awareness as the most important thing.

[83] The words of the thirty-seven heap mandala offering.

[84] The system of this text is the Longchen Nyingthig system of Chod.

of the accumulation tree. In this case, there can be a clear visualization which is part of a good practice, and an unclear one, and so on —there are various possibilities.[85]

4. Guru Yoga

You visualize Orgyan Vajradhara in the space before yourself and all other sentient beings. His nature is that he contains all the root and lineage gurus and he is wearing the accoutrements of an heruka.[86] Then you and all other sentient beings supplicate him unanimously from the very cores of your hearts. At the end, you think that the root guru's three secrets and your three doors[87] become many in one taste then set yourself in equipoise on the state of actuality.[88] Up to here has been the preliminaries. Now for the main part.

---

[85] In this system, there is less emphasis on the outer aspect of the practice. This system goes straight to the heart of the practice which is the elimination of self-cherishing based on the view and the offering done on the basis of that. Thus, in this system the visualization is not the main point. In this system there are many possibilities: you could have a clear visualization together with good or bad practice; an unclear visualization together with good or bad practice; and so on.

[86] The accoutrements of an heruka are the six symbolic ornaments. They are explained in detail in the *Illuminator Tibetan-English Dictionary*.

[87] The guru's three secrets are his enlightened body, speech, and mind. Your three doors are your ordinary body, speech, and mind.

[88] One khenpo said to me, "… in the state of actuality, Dzogpa Chenpo" but then corrected himself and said, "Well, as would be said in the Chod system of teaching, '… in the state of actuality, Prajnaparamita'". Each system does have its own terminology and own way of expressing the teaching, as was explained in the introduction.

2. Main Part

The main part consists of: separating awareness from matter then creating the Wrathful Woman; inviting the guests; and doing the three or four great distributions.[89]

1. Creation of the Wrathful Woman

You recite the words like these, "This body gross due to being well fed and fattened, young and tender, has clearly visible in its heart centre the essence of my own mind, Machig Black Wrathful Woman, dancing".[90] You exclaim PHAṬ which causes her to be sent out through your Brahma aperture, up into space. Using the flaying knife in her hand, she slices off your skull at the level of the point between the eye brows, takes it in her left hand, then puts it on a hearth of three skulls each of which is as large as Mt. Meru. The skull has the area of a third-order thousandfold world system. She uses the flaying knife to cut up your body, bit by bit, into pieces which she puts into the skullcup. Then, underneath the skullcup, a wind stirs that fans the fire and makes it blaze. Blood, flesh, and bones all three are melted and thereby changed into the nature of amṛita. That is blessed with OṂ, ĀḤ, and HŪṂ. This part of the visualization is done as taught in the main texts.[91]

[89] The distributions are sometimes enumerated as three and sometimes as four.

[90] Dza Patrul says "words like these" because he does not give an exact quote from Jigmey Lingpa's text but words similar to that with a little embellishment to provide more information.

[91] The author is saying that you can get more information about the process by looking it up in other texts of the general system of Chod. The process is described further in the previous commentary.

2. Calling up the Guests

Light rays from the heart centre of yourself, Wrathful Woman, summon first the higher being guests of the offering—the gurus, yidams, dakinis, buddhas, bodhisatvas, and so on—then after that, the lower being guests of the offering—gods, demons, dons, and obstructors. All of them assemble, filling the entire space of the sky. Think that then recite the section "Recipients of offering, the three roots and samaya'd ones …"

3. The Visualization of the Great Distribution

First you must know the visualizations of the distributions, as follows.[92] All classes of guests in general will be invited to both the white distribution and the multicoloured distribution. In particular, the classes who eat flesh and blood will be invited to the red distribution, the dons and obstructors will be given the black distribution, and so on. Then you join that knowledge to the liturgy of our system as follows. The higher being guests are given the white distribution in the nature of amṛita. The lower being guests of gods, demons, dons, obstructors, elemental spirits, pretas, rakshas[93], and so on have the red distribution dedicated to them in the form of the three things of flesh, blood, and bones. Beings within the six classes other than yourself with whom you have karmic debts and retribu-

---

[92] First, you have to learn the various distributions as explained in the various main texts of Chod. Then you need to apply that general knowledge to the specific ways of doing the distributions which are set out in the Longchen Nyingthig text.

[93] Elemental spirits are usually a less troublesome type of spirit who live with the elements, for example tree spirits. Pretas are the class of hungry ghosts who have the power to enter the human realm and cause paranormal events; they are of varying capability all the way through to being very dangerous. Rakshas are vicious, flesh-eating spirits who live in this human world, like the trolls of European lore.

tions are given, in the multicoloured distribution, whatever they specifically want in the form of a rain of desirable things, and so on. The details of the various visualizations can be known from the main and instructional texts of Chod.[94]

3. Conclusion

For the conclusion, dedications and prayers of aspiration are done. The very meaningful activities of exchanging oneself for other with Sending and Taking, performing generosity through the generosity of giving dharma, and so on are to be practised in accordance with the general, main path of the conquerors' sons. Similarly, the practice of giving away the body is done in six or four sessions, etcetera.

When you do the practice, the central point is as follows. The dualistic minds which conceive of the body as something very dear and which grasp at a self will be brought forth and exposed. When that happens you think, "Whoever wants it, take it! Let whatever happens, happen!", and at the same time preserve the state of the view that cuts the fetters of the I that comes with the thinker of that thought. Joining compassion to that emptiness, you should make the development of the samadhis of the four immeasurable ones your primary concern.

This "Cutting" is to be engaged by practising the mother, the mind of factual prajnaparamita, which itself is emptiness with a core of compassion. Therefore, the main thing is to do the practice with

---

[94] The main texts of Chod will give explanations which are generally applicable. The instructional texts, meaning the instructional texts of our Nyingthig system, will give details appropriate to this system, for example, Dza Patrul's *Words of My Perfect Teacher* contains an explanation of the various distributions as done in this system.

great compassion and then, within that, it is important that you do it with a peaceful, tamed, and attentive approach.

Then there is the point that, however much you do the practice, it should produce merit and should have the capacity to do something for the welfare of god and demon migrators. Anything other than that, such as looking about with eyes of anger whilst having the idea that you will beat up and expel any gods and demons that you do find is Chod gone wrong; it can be known from the authoritative statements of Machig, and so on that such Chod is the work of maras and will lead you to the bad migrations. With that kind of cutting, whether you work at the purifications of the preliminaries or do the practice of the main part, either way, not the slightest experience of the practice will arise in you. Then, because you have not made great compassion part of your practice, when you do go to terrifying places and the like, the gods and demons will get to you first and manipulate your mind to make what seem to be extra perceptions, speech capabilities, and so forth happen to you but these will not be the real ones. If that happens, these seeming capabilities will arise but your mindstream will actually be becoming further removed from dharma. You must understand that a person who becomes highly accomplished in such types of experience will be one who cries out, "Oh no!" and falls into a major faint when he reaches the gates of the city of hell.

Therefore, at all times and in all circumstances, have faith in the guru and Three Jewels that thinks, "Think of me!"[95] And have raw

[95] This is a standard way in Tibetan of speaking of someone who has unshakeable conviction in the guru and Three Jewels. Such as person constantly has his mind connected with the guru and Three Jewels and is constantly asking them to pay attention to him.

compassion[96] for sentient beings of the six classes. And, within the state which does not part from imposing the face of equalization of taste onto the concepts of hope and fear[97], work at the practice of casting aside your body as food. And, assiduously do both a practice of generosity of dharma which is connected with the conquerors' command[98] and prayers of aspiration that arrange merit for those with whom you have connected. And, cut the five poisons of the mindstreams of both yourself and others that come from holding the gods and demons very dear compared to yourself. Doing it that way is the un-mistaken, good path of the practice of Chod which delights the conquerors together with their sons.

> Through the kindness of many matchless holy ones
> I've drunk the nectar of obtaining empowerment which has been very satisfying but
> When I've tried to gain experience, I've had no success; I'm of low fortune!
> Still, I think, "With the mastery that I do have of the profound meaning's foremost instructions that have been explained to me,
> This humble person is fortunate isn't he

---

[96] A more modern edition of the text has this metaphoric wording changed to "uncontrived" compassion but the original text is correct. "Raw compassion" is a way of speaking in Dza Patrul's East Tibetan dialect that means uncontrived compassion.

[97] Equalization of taste means seeing that any given appearance is not different from another because all appearances are marked with emptiness. Equalization of taste is not a conceptual approach, it is a practice in which emptiness is actually mixed with appearances. In this practice, the hope and fear engendered by acts of provocation have the actual experience or the face of appearance-emptiness imposed on them.

[98] "Connected with the conqueror's command" means as taught by Shakyamuni Buddha in the sutra teachings.

Compared to the old dog Chod practitioners who have been manipulated by the savage maras
That lie in wait behind the path which pleases the conquerors
Here at this ending period of the era of the dregs?!"[99]
Now that is part of the lord guru's kindness, too;
To repay that kindness I remind myself, "Samsara is limitless",
And, with the yearning borne of faith that never forgets the dharma lord,
I supplicate him again and again to please bless me![100]

This *Chod Practice Sound of Dakini Laughter* which has been explained above itself clearly shows our system. Then, in particular, there are the main, instructional, thorough explanation, and so on texts, of both the lord who has accomplished glory, Vajrapani, and

---

[99] Dza Patrul is saying that has not been able to gain deep experience by practising but even then he has had the fortune to obtain the profound foremost instructions of the lineage because they have kept him pointed in the right direction and prevented him from making the major errors that many of the old dog Chod practitioners have fallen into. With this, he is making a point of how powerful the foremost instructions of this Nyingthig Great Completion are compared to the lesser oral instructions that come with general Chod. This same point is made in the introduction of this book. Note how this also fits with the title of his text which is "The Foremost Instructions ..."

[100] His good fortune is a kindness coming from the foremost instructions of the lineage and especially a kindness of his guru who provided them to him. Therefore, he remembers his guru's kindness and asks for his blessings.

his chief son Aryadeva[101]. After that, in particular, there are the many written works, extensive and condensed, concerned with bringing others under one's control and subjugation.[102] Taken together, they are like a lake of water with the eight qualities so there is no need for me to dig out a salty well right on the banks of such a lake![103] Nonetheless, I cannot go against the command of those who pressed me to write about this, so I have, like a deaf man writing music, written down this explanation of dharma of which I have no experience.

Virtue! Virtue! Virtue!

---

[101] These are the texts on the emptiness of the Prajnaparamita teachings written by Nagarjuna and his main disciple Aryadeva, which form the basis for the view of Chod.

[102] The texts specifically on the practice of Chod.

[103] Water of the eight qualities is the finest water that can be found in the human realm. The eight qualities are listed in the *Illuminator Tibetan-English Dictionary*.

Glossary of Terms

Actuality, Tib. gnas lugs: A key term in both sutra and tantra and one of a pair of terms, the other being "apparent reality" (Tib. snang lugs). The two terms are used when determining the reality of a situation. The actuality of any given situation is how (lugs) the situation actuality sits or is present (gnas); the apparent reality is how (lugs) any given situation appears (snang) to an observer. Something could appear in many different ways, depending on the circumstances at the time and on the being perceiving it but, regardless of those circumstances, it will always have its own actuality of how it really is. This term is frequently used in Mahamudra and Great Completion teachings to mean the fundamental reality of any given phenomenon or situation before any deluded mind alters it and makes it appear differently.

Affliction, Skt. kleśha, Tib. nyon mongs: This term is usually translated as emotion or disturbing emotion, etcetera, but the Buddha was very specific about the meaning of this word. When the Buddha referred to the emotions, meaning a movement of mind, he did not refer to them as such but called them "klesha" in Sanskrit, meaning exactly "affliction". It is a basic part of the Buddhist teaching that emotions afflict beings, giving them problems at the time and causing more problems in the future.

Alaya, Skt. ālaya, Tib. kun gzhi: This term, if translated, is usually translated as all-base or something similar. It is a Sanskrit term that means a range that underlies and forms a basis for something else. In Buddhist teaching, it means a particular level of mind that sits beneath all other levels of mind. However, it is used in several different ways in the Buddhist teaching and changes to a different meaning in each case. In the Great Completion teachings, an important distinction is made between alaya alone and alaya consciousness.

Appearance and becoming, Tib. snang srid: This is a stock phrase in which "appearance" refers to the worlds that appear to the senses of beings and "becoming" refers to the beings born into those worlds. "Becoming" actually means "a birth taken somewhere with the result that a being becomes one type of migrator or another". This phrase "appearance and becoming" is equivalent in meaning to another stock phrase "containers and contents" with the containers being the appearances of their worlds and contents being the beings in those worlds. The phrase often is used indicate all of samsara and nirvana, though it can be used to indicate only one or the other.

Arousing the mind, Tib. sems bskyed: This is a technical term nearly always used to mean "arousing the enlightenment mind", although it can be used to refer to the deliberate production of other types of mind, for example renunciation. There are two types of arousing the enlightenment mind—fictional and superfactual; see under fictional enlightenment mind and superfactual enlightenment mind.

Assurance, Tib. gdeng: Although often translated as confidence, this term means assurance with all of the extra meaning conveyed by that term. A bird might be confident of its ability to fly but, more than that, it has the assurance that it will not fall to the ground because it knows it has wings and it has the training to use them. Similarly, a person might be confident that he could liberate the afflictions but not be assured of doing so because of lack of training or other causes. However, a person who has accumulated the causes to be able to liberate afflictions is assured of the ability to do so.

Becoming(s), Skt. bhāvana, Tib. srid pa: This is another name for samsaric existence. Beings in samsara have a samsaric existence but, more than that, they are constantly in a state of becoming—becoming this type of being or that type of being in this abode or that, as they are driven along without choice by the karmic process that drives samsaric existence.

Clinging, Tib. zhen pa: In Buddhism, this term refers specifically to the twofold process of dualistic mind mis-taking things that are not true, not pure, etcetera as true, pure, etcetera and then, because of seeing them as highly desirable even though they are not, attaching itself to or clinging to those things. This type of clinging acts as a kind of glue that keeps a person joined to the unsatisfactory things of cyclic existence because of mistakenly seeing them as desirable.

Complete purity, Tib. rnam dag: This term refers to the quality of a buddha's mind, which is completely pure compared to a sentient being's mind. The mind of a being in samsara has its primordially pure nature covered over by the muck of dualistic mind. If the being practises correctly, the impurity can be removed and mind can be returned to its original state of complete purity.

Concept label, Tib. mtshan ma. This is the technical name for the conceptual constructs that function as the words of conceptual mind's language. For example, you could see a table in direct visual perception of table in which case there would be no concept labels involved or you could think "table" in an inferential or conceptual perception of table in which case there is a label "table" used whenever the table is referenced. The label or name tag is the conceptual token.

Although we usually reference phenomena via these concepts, the phenomena are not the dualistically referenced things we think of them as being. The actual fact of the phenomena is quite different from the labels used to think about them and is known by wisdom rather than concept-based dualistic mind. Therefore, this term is often used in Buddhist literature to signify that samsaric mind is involved rather than non-dualistic wisdom.

Confusion, Tib. 'khrul pa: In Buddhism, this term mostly refers to the fundamental confusion of taking things the wrong way that happens because of fundamental ignorance, although it can also have the more general meaning of having lots of thoughts and being confused about it. In the first case, it is defined like this "Confusion is the appearance to rational mind of something being present when it is not" and refers, for example, to seeing an object, such as a table, as being truly present, when in fact it is present only as mere, interdependent appearance.

Contrived, contrivance, Tib. bcos pa: A term meaning that something has been altered from its native state.

Dharmadhatu, Skt. dharmadhātu, Tib. chos kyi dbyings: A *dhātu* is a place or basis from or within which something can come into being. In the case of a dharma dhātu, it is the place or space which is a basis from and in which all dharmas or phenomena, can and do come into being. If a flower bed is the place where flowers grow and are found, the dharmadhātu is the dharma or phenomena bed in which all phenomena come into being and are found. The term is used in all levels of Buddhist teaching with that general meaning but the explanation of it becomes more profound as the teaching becomes more profound. For example, in Great Completion and Mahāmudrā, it is the all-pervading sphere of luminosity-wisdom, given that luminosity is where phenomena arise and luminosity is none other than wisdom.

Dharmakaya, Skt. dharmakāya, Tib. chos sku: In the general teachings of Buddhism, this refers to the mind of a buddha, with "dharma" meaning reality and "kaya" meaning body. In the Thorough Cut practice of Great Completion it additionally has the special meaning of being the means by which one rapidly imposes liberation on oneself.

Discursive thought, Skt. vikalpita, Tib. rnam rtog: This means more than just the superficial thought that is heard as a voice in the head. It includes the entirety of conceptual process that arises due to mind contacting any object of any of the senses. The Sanskrit and Tibetan literally mean "(dualistic) thought (that arises from the mind wandering among the) various (superficies *q.v.* perceived in the doors of the senses)".

Don(s), Tib. gdon: A general term for any kind of negative force that hits a person and brings trouble. It could be any external or internal thing that causes trouble. A good way to think of it is "negative influence" or "negative force".

Elaboration, Tib. spro ba: This is a general name for what is given off by dualistic mind as it goes about its conceptual business. The term is pejorative in that it implies that a story has been made up, unnecessarily, about something which is actually nothing, which is empty. Elaborations, because of what they are, prevent a person from seeing emptiness directly.

Enlightenment mind, Skt. bodhicitta, Tib. byang chub sems: This is a key term of the Great Vehicle. It is the type of mind that is connected not with the lesser enlightenment of an arhat but with the enlightenment of a truly complete buddha. As such, it is a mind which is connected with the aim of bringing all sentient beings to that same level of buddhahood. A person who has engendered this mind has by definition entered the Great Vehicle and is either a bodhisatva or a buddha.

It is important to understand that "enlightenment mind" is used to refer equally to the minds of all levels of bodhisatva on the path to buddhahood and to the mind of a buddha who has completed the path. Therefore, it is not "mind striving for enlightenment" as is so often translated, but "enlightenment mind", meaning that kind of mind which is connected with the full enlightenment of a truly complete buddha and which is present in all those who belong to the Great Vehicle. The term is used in the conventional Great Vehicle and also in the Vajra Vehicle. In the Vajra Vehicle, there are some special uses of the term where substances of the pure aspect of the subtle physical body are understood to be manifestations of enlightenment mind.

Entity, Tib. ngo bo: The entity of something is just exactly what that thing is. In English we would often simply say "thing" rather than entity. However, in Buddhism, "thing" has a very specific meaning rather than the general meaning that it has in English. It has become common to translate this term as "essence" *q.v.* However, in most cases "entity", meaning what a thing is rather than an essence of that thing, is the correct translation for this term.

Essence, Tib. ngo bo: This is a key term used throughout Buddhist theory. The original in Sanskrit and the term in Tibetan, too, has both meanings of "essence" and "entity". In some situations the term has more the first meaning and in others, the second. For example, when speaking of mind and mind's essence, it is referring to the core or essential part within mind. On the other hand, when speaking of something such as fire, one can speak of the entity, fire, and its characteristics, such as heat, and so on; in this case, the term does not mean essence but means that thing, what it actually is. See also under entity.

Expanse, Skt. dhātu, Tib. dbyings: The Sanskrit term has over twenty meanings. Many of those meanings are also present in the Tibetan equivalent. In the Vajra Vehicle teachings it is used as a replacement for the term emptiness that conveys a non-theoretical sense of the experience of emptiness. When used this way, it has the sense "expanse" because emptiness is experienced as an expanse in which all phenomena appear. It is frequently an abbreviation of dharmadhatu.

Fictional, Skt. saṃvṛti, Tib. kun rdzob: This term is paired with the term "superfactual" *q.v.* In the past, these terms have been translated as "relative" and "absolute" respectively, but those translations are nothing like the original terms. These terms are extremely important in the Buddhist teaching so it is very important that they be corrected, but more than that, if the actual meaning of these terms is not presented, then the teaching connected with them cannot be understood.

The Sanskrit term samvrtti means a deliberate invention, a fiction, a hoax. It refers to the mind of ignorance which, because of being obscured and so not seeing suchness, is not true but a fiction. The things that appear to that ignorance are therefore fictional. Nonetheless, the beings who live in this ignorance believe that the things that appear to them through the filter of ignorance are true, are real. Therefore, these beings live in fictional truth.

Fictional truth, Skt. saṃvṛtisatya, Tib. kun rdzob bden pa: See under "Fictional" for an explanation of this term.

Fictional truth enlightenment mind, Tib. kun rdzob bden pa'i byang chub sems: One of a pair of terms explained in the Great Vehicle; the other is Superfactual Truth Enlightenment Mind. See under fictional truth and superfactual truth for information about those terms. Enlightenment mind is defined as two types. The fictional type is the conventional type: it is explained as consisting of love and great compassion within the framework of an intention to obtain truly complete enlightenment for the sake of all sentient beings. The superfactual truth type is the ultimate type: it is explained as the enlightenment mind that is directly perceiving emptiness.

Foci, focus, focus on, Tib. gtad so: A focus is any given thing that a dualistic mind has focussed on. Having a focus is equivalent to having a reference *q.v.*, and focussing on a focus entails referencing a reference. All of these terms imply the presence of dualistic mind.

Foremost instruction, Skt. upadeśha, Tib. man ngag: There are several types of instruction mentioned in Buddhist literature: there is the general level of instruction which is the meaning contained in the words of the texts of the tradition; on a more personal and direct level there is oral instruction which has been passed down from teacher to student from the time of the buddha; and on the most profound level there are foremost instructions which are not only oral instructions provided by one's guru but are special, core instructions that come out of personal experience and which convey the teaching concisely and with the full weight of personal experience. Foremost instructions are crucial to the Vajra Vehicle because these are the special way of passing on the profound instructions needed for the student's realization.

Grasped-grasping, Tib. gzung 'dzin: When mind is turned outwardly as it is in the normal operation of dualistic mind, it has developed two faces that appear simultaneously. Special names are given to these two faces: mind appearing in the form of the external object being referenced is called "that which is grasped" and mind appearing in the form of the consciousness that is registering it is called the "grasper" or "grasping" of it. Thus, there is the pair of terms "grasped-grasper" or "grasped-grasping". When these two terms are used, it alerts one to the fact that a Mind Only style of presentation is being discussed. This pair of terms pervades Mind Only, Middle Way, and tantric writings and is exceptionally important in all of them.

Note that one could substitute the word "apprehended" for "grasped" and "apprehender" for "grasper" or "grasping" and that would reflect one connotation of the original Sanskrit terminology. The solidified duality of grasped and grasper is nothing but an invention of dualistic thought; it has that kind of character or characteristic.

Great Completion, rdzogs pa chen po: Two main practices of reality developed in the Buddhist traditions of ancient India and then came to Tibet: Great Completion (Mahasandhi) and Great Seal (Mahamudra). Great Completion and Great Seal are names for reality and names for a practice that directly leads to that reality. Their ways of describing reality and their practices are very similar. The Great Completion teachings are the pinnacle teachings of the tantric teachings of Buddhism that first came into Tibet with Padmasambhava and his peers and were later kept alive in the Nyingma (Earlier Ones) tradition. The Great Seal practice came into Tibet later and was held in the Sakya and Kagyu lineages. Later again, the Great Seal was held by the Gelugpa lineage, which obtained its transmissions of the instructions from the Sakya and Kagyu lineages.

It is popular nowadays to call Great Completion by the name Great Perfection, though that is a mistake. The original name Mahasandhi refers to that one space of reality in which all things come together. Thus it means "completeness" or "completion" as the Tibetans chose to translate it and does not imply or contain the sense of "perfection".

Great Vehicle, Skt. mahāyāna, Tib. theg pa chen po: The Buddha's teachings as a whole can be summed up into three vehicles where a vehicle is defined as that which can carry a person to a certain destination. The first vehicle, called the Lesser Vehicle, contains the teachings designed to get an individual moving on the spiritual path through showing the unsatisfactory state of cyclic existence and an emancipation from that. However, that path is only concerned with personal emancipation and fails to take account of all of the beings that there are in existence. There used to be eighteen schools of Lesser Vehicle in India but the only one surviving nowadays is the Theravada of south-east Asia. The Greater Vehicle is a step up from that. The Buddha explained that it was great in comparison to the Lesser Vehicle for seven reasons. The first of those is that it is concerned with attaining the truly complete enlightenment of a truly complete buddha for the sake of every sentient being where the Lesser Vehicle is concerned only with a personal liberation that is not truly complete enlightenment and which is achieved only for the sake of that practitioner. The Great Vehicle has two divisions: a conventional form in which the path is taught in a logical, conventional way, and an unconventional form in which the path is taught in a very direct way. This latter vehicle is called the Vajra Vehicle because it takes the innermost, indestructible (vajra) fact of reality of one's own mind as the vehicle to enlightenment.

Introduction and To Introduce, Tib. ngos sprad and ngos sprod pa respectively: This pair of terms is usually mistakenly translated today as "pointing out" and "to point out. The terms are the standard terms used in day to day life for the situation in which one person introduces another person to someone or something. They are the exact same words as our English "introduction" and "to introduce".

In the Vajra Vehicle, these terms are specifically used for the situation in which one person introduces another person to the nature of his own mind. There is a term in Tibetan for "pointing out", but that term is never used for this purpose because in this case no one points out anything. Rather, a person is introduced by another person to a part of himself that he has forgotten about.

Latency, Skt. vāsanā, Tib. bag chags: The original Sanskrit has the meaning exactly of "latency". The Tibetan term translates that inexactly with "something sitting there (Tib. chags) within the environment of mind (Tib. bag)". Although it has become popular to translate this term into English with "habitual pattern", that is not its meaning. The term refers to a karmic seed that has been imprinted on the mindstream and is present there as a latency, ready and waiting to come into manifestation.

Liveliness, Tib. rtsal: This is a key term in both Mahāmudrā and Great Completion. The term is sometimes translated as "display" or "expression" but neither is correct. The primary meaning is the ability of something to express itself but in use, the actual expression of that ability is also included. Thus, in English it would not be "expression" but "expressivity" but that is too dry. This term is not at all dry; it is talking about the life of something and how that life comes into expression; "liveliness" fits the meaning of the original term very well.

Luminosity or illumination, Skt. prabhāsvara, Tib. 'od gsal ba: The essence of mind has two aspects: an emptiness factor and a knowing factor. The Buddha and many Indian religious teachers used "luminosity" as a metaphor for the knowing quality of the essence of mind. If in English we would say "Mind has a knowing quality", the teachers of ancient India would say, "Mind has an illuminative quality; it is like a source of light which illuminates what it knows".

This term has been translated as "clear light" but that is a mistake that comes from not understanding the etymology of the word. It does not refer to a light that has the quality of clearness (something that makes no sense, actually!) but to the illuminative property which is the nature of the empty mind.

Note also that in both Sanskrit and Tibetan Buddhist literature, this term is frequently abbreviated just to Skt. "vara" and Tib. "gsal ba" with no change of meaning. Unfortunately, this has been thought to be another word and it has then been translated with "clarity", when in fact it is just this term in abbreviation.

Lustre, Tib. mdangs: In both Mahamudra and Great Completion there is the general term "output" (Tib. gdangs) meaning what is given off by something, for example the sound given off by a loudspeaker. There is another Tibetan word spelled "mdangs" instead of "gdangs". The Mahamudra teaching makes no difference between the two terms but Great Completion teachings does make a distinction. In great completion this term spelled "mdangs" has the special meaning not of the general output coming from something but of the "lustre" of thing. It is a more subtle meaning. In Great Completion it conveys not just the sense of what is given off by the emptiness factor of mind in general (which would be its output and which is talked about, too) but specifically means the lustre of the emptiness or, you could also say, its lustre.

Mara, Skt. māra, Tib. bdud: The Sanskrit term is closely related to the word "death". Buddha spoke of four classes of extremely negative influences that have the capacity to drag a sentient being deep into samsara. They are the "maras" or "kiss of death" of: having a samsaric set of five skandhas; having afflictions; death itself; and the son of gods, which means being seduced and taken in totally by sensuality.

Meteoric iron, Tib. gnam lcags: Meteoric iron is a misnomer. See under sky iron.

Mind, Skt. chitta, Tib. sems: There are several terms for mind in the Buddhist tradition, each with its own, specific meaning. This term is the most general term for the samsaric type of mind. It refers to the type of mind that is produced because of fundamental ignorance of enlightened mind. Whereas the wisdom of enlightened mind lacks all complexity and knows in a non-dualistic way, this mind of un-enlightenment is a very complicated apparatus that only ever knows in a dualistic way.

The Mahamudra and Great Completion teachings use the terms "entity of mind" and "mind's entity" to refer to what this complicated, samsaric mind is at core—the enlightened form of mind.

Not stopped, Tib. ma 'gags pa: An important path term in the teaching of both Mahamudra and Great Completion. There are two ways to explain this term: according to view and to practice. The following explanation is of the latter type. The core of mind has two parts—emptiness and luminosity—which are in fact unified so must come that way in practice. However, a practitioner who is still on the path will fall into one extreme or the other and that results in "stoppage" of the expression of the luminosity. When emptiness and luminosity are unified in practice, there is no stoppage of the expression of the luminosity that comes from having fallen into one extreme or the other. Thus "non-stopped luminosity" is a term that indicates that there is the luminosity with all of its appearance yet that luminosity, for the practitioner, is not mistaken, is not stopped off. "Stopped luminosity" is an experience like luminosity but in which the appearances have, at least to some extent, not been mixed with emptiness.

Outflow, Skt. āsrāva, Tib. zag pa: The Sanskrit term means a bad discharge, like pus coming out of a wound. Outflows occur when wisdom loses its footing and falls into the elaborations of dualistic mind. Therefore, anything with duality also has outflows. This is sometimes translated as "defiled" or "conditioned" but these fail to capture the meaning. The idea is that wisdom can remain self-contained in its own unique sphere but, when it loses its ability to stay within itself, it starts to have leakages into dualism that are defilements on the wisdom. See also under un-outflowed.

Output, Tib. gdangs: Output is a general term for that which is given off by something, for example, the sound that comes from a loudspeaker. In Mahamudra and Great Completion, it refers to what is given off by the emptiness factor of the essence of mind. Emptiness is the empty condition of the essence of mind, like space. However, that emptiness has liveliness which comes off the emptiness as compassion and all the other qualities of enlightened mind, and, equally, all the apparatus of dualistic mind. All of this is called its output. Note that the Great Completion teachings have a special word that is a more refined version of this term; see under complexion for that.

Poisons, Tib. dug: In Buddhism, poison is a general term for the afflictions. For samsaric beings, the afflictions are poisonous things which harm them. The Buddha most commonly spoke of the three poisons, which are the principal afflictions of desire, aggression, and ignorance. He also spoke of "the five poisons" which is a slightly longer enumeration of the principal afflictions: desire, aggression, delusion, pride, and jealousy.

Prajna, Skt. prajñā, Tib. shes rab: The Sanskrit term, literally meaning "best type of mind" is defined as that which makes correct distinctions between this and that and hence which arrives at correct understanding. It has been translated as "wisdom" but that is not correct because it is, generally speaking, a mental event belonging to dualistic mind where "wisdom" is used to refer to the non-dualistic knower of a buddha. Moreover, the main feature of prajña is its ability to distinguish correctly between one thing and another and hence to arrive at a correct understanding.

Preserve, Tib. skyong ba: This term is important in both Mahamudra and Great Completion. In general, it means to defend, protect, nurture, maintain. In the higher tantras it means to keep something just as it is, to nurture that something so that it stays and is not lost. Also, in the higher tantras, it is often used in reference to preserving the state where the state is some particular state of being. Because of this, the phrase "preserve the state" is an important instruction in the higher tantras.

Rational mind, Tib. blo: Tib. blo: Rational mind is one of several terms for mind in Buddhist terminology. It specifically refers to a mind that judges this against that. It is mainly used to refer to samsaric mind, given that samsaric mind only works in the dualistic mode of comparing this versus that. Because of this, the term is mainly used in a pejorative sense to point out samsaric mind as opposed to a non-dualistic enlightened type of mind. However, it is occasionally used to refer to the discriminating wisdom aspect of non-dualistic mind, for example, in the case of a buddha. In that case it is a mind making distinctions between this and that but within the context of non-dualistic wisdom.

This term has been commonly translated simply as "mind" but that fails to identify it properly and leaves it confused with the many other words that are also translated simply as "mind". It is not just another mind but is specifically the sort of mind that creates the situation of this and that (*ratio* in Latin). Therefore, the term "rational mind" fits perfectly. This is a key term which must be understood as a specific term with a specific meaning and should not be just glossed over as "mind".

Reference and Referencing, Tib. dmigs pa: Referencing is the name for the process in which dualistic mind references an actual object by using a conceptual label instead of the actual object. Whatever is referenced is then called a reference. Note that these terms imply the presence of dualistic mind and their opposites, non-referencing and being without reference, imply the presence of non-dualistic wisdom.

Refuge, Skt. śharaṇaṃ, Tib. bskyab pa: The Sanskrit term means "shelter", "protection from harm". Everyone seeks a refuge from the unsatisfactoriness of life, even if it is a simple act like brushing the teeth to prevent the body from decaying un-necessarily. Buddhists, after having thought carefully about their situation and who could provide a refuge from it which would be thoroughly reliable, find that three things—buddha, dharma, and sangha—are the only things that could provide that kind of refuge. Therefore, Buddhists take refuge in those Three Jewels of Refuge as they are called. Taking refuge in the Three Jewels is clearly laid out as the one doorway to all Buddhist practice and realization.

Rigpa, Skt. vidyā, Tib. rig pa: This is the singularly most important term in the whole of Great Completion and Mahamudra. In particular, it is the key word of all words in the Great Completion system of the Thorough Cut. Rigpa literally means to know in the sense of "I see!" It is used at all levels of meaning from the coarsest everyday sense of knowing something to the deepest sense of knowing something as presented in the system of Thorough Cut. The system of Thorough Cut uses this term in a very special sense, though it still retains its basic meaning of "to know". To translate it as "awareness", which is common practice today, is a poor practice; there are many kinds of awareness but there is only one rigpa and besides, rigpa is substantially more than just awareness. Since this is such an important term and since it lacks an equivalent in English, I choose not to translate it.

This is the term used to indicate enlightened mind as experienced by the practitioner on the path of these practices. The term itself specifically refers to the dynamic knowing quality of mind. It absolutely does not mean a simple registering, as implied by the word "awareness" which unfortunately is often used to translate this term. There is no word in English that exactly matches it, though the idea of "seeing" or "insight on the spot" is very close. Proof of this is found in the fact that the original Sanskrit term "vidya" is actually the root of all words in English that start with "vid" and mean "to see", for example, "video", "vision", and so on. Chogyam Trungpa Rinpoche, who was particularly skilled at getting Tibetan words into English, also stated that this term rigpa really did not have a good equivalent in English, though he thought that "insight" was the closest. My own conclusion after hearing extensive teaching on it is that rigpa is best left untranslated. Note that rigpa has both noun and verb forms.

Self-arising wisdom, Tib. rang byung ye shes: The words "self-arising" are added to wisdom *q.v.* to indicate that it is not caused, that it is outside the samsaric process of cause and effect. As the vidyadhara Chogyam Trungpa said, it is self-existing.

Shamatha, Skt. śhamatha, Tib. gzhi gnas: This is the name of one of the two main practices of meditation used in the Buddhist system to gain insight into reality. This practice creates a one-pointedness of mind which can then be used as a foundation for development of the insight of the other practice, vipashyana. If the development of śhamatha is taken through to completion, the result is a mind that sits stable on its object without any effort and a body which is filled with ease. Altogether, this result of the practice is called "the creation of workability of body and mind".

Sky iron, Tib. gnam lcags: Although this is usually translated as "meteoric iron", that is a mistake. The Tibetan name means "sky iron". Well-educated Tibetans who know the difference between the two state categorically that this term refers to a kind of metal that falls to earth at the times of particular intense lightning strikes. According to Tibetan culture, particularly violent thunderbolts come down with this metal and also with very strong acid. The metal buries itself underground where it stays for several years before emerging. When it does emerge, it often has shapes such as vajras and so on associated with it. The translation of this term with "meteoric iron" has led Western practitioners to a general belief that this is talking about iron obtained from actual meteorites but Tibetan tradition does not think of it that way. The key point is that it is said to have very powerful and sometimes miraculous qualities.

State, Tib. ngang: This is a key term in Mahamudra and Great Completion. Unfortunately it is often not translated and in so doing much meaning is lost. Alternatively, it is often translated as "within" which is incorrect. The term means a "state". A state is a certain, ongoing situation. In Buddhist meditation in general, there are various states that a practitioner has to enter and remain in as part of developing the meditation.

Superfactual, Skt. paramārtha, Tib. don dam: This term is paired with the term "fictional" *q.v.* In the past, the terms have been translated as "relative" and "absolute", but those translations are nothing like the original terms. These terms are extremely important in the Buddhist teaching so it is very important that their translations be corrected but, more than that, if the actual meaning of these terms is not presented, the teaching connected with them cannot be understood.

The Sanskrit term paramartha literally means "the fact for that which is above all others, special, superior" and refers to what is known to the wisdom mind possessed by those who have developed themselves spiritually to the point of having transcended samsara. That wisdom is *superior* to an ordinary, un-developed person's consciousness and the *facts* that appear on its surface are superior compared to the facts that appear on the ordinary person's consciousness. Therefore, it is superfact or, more colloquially, the highest thing that could be known. What this wisdom knows is true for the beings who have it, therefore what the wisdom sees is superfactual truth.

Superfactual truth, Skt. paramārthasatya, Tib. don dam bden pa: See under superfactual.

Superfactual truth enlightenment mind, Tib. don dam bden pa'i byang chub sems: This is one of a pair of terms; the other is Fictional Truth Enlightenment Mind *q.v.* for explanation.

Temporary experience, Tib. nyams: The practice of meditation brings with it various experiences that happen simply because of doing meditation. These experiences are temporary experiences and not the final, unchanging experience, of realization.

Third-order thousandfold world system, Tib. stong gsum 'jig rten: Indian cosmology has for its smallest cosmic unit a single Mt. Meru with four continents type of world system; an analogy might be a single planetary system like our solar system. One thousand of those makes a first-order thousandfold world system; an analogy might be a galaxy. One thousand of those makes a second-order thousandfold world system; an analogy might be a region of space with many galaxies. One thousand of those makes a third-order thousandfold world system (1000 raised to the power 3); an analogy would be one whole universe like ours. The Buddha said that there were countless numbers of third order thousandfold world systems, each of which would be roughly equivalent to a universe like ours.

Three secrets, Tib. gsang ba: This term is usually defined as a path term which refers to the body, speech, and mind of a person who is on the way to buddhahood. When a person becomes a buddha, he has reached his full state of enlightenment and at that point the three secrets have become unchanging so are now referred to with what is defined as a fruition term, "the three vajras" of a tathagata.

Uncontrived, Tib. ma bcos pa: The opposite of "contrived". Something which has not been altered from its native state; something which has been left just as it is.

Un-outflowed, Skt. anāśhrāva, Tib. zag pa med pa: Un-outflowed dharmas are ones that are connected with wisdom that has not lost its footing and leaked out into a defiled state; it is self-contained wisdom without any taint of dualistic mind and its apparatus. See also outflowed.

Un-stopped, Tib. ma 'gags pa: An important path term in the teaching of both Mahamudra and Great Completion. The essence of mind has two parts: emptiness and luminosity. Both of these must come unified. However, when a practitioner does the practice, he will fall into one extreme or the other and that is called "stoppage". The aim of the practice is to get to the stage in which there is both emptiness and luminosity together. In that case, there is no stoppage of falling into one extreme or the other. Thus non-stopped luminosity is a term that indicates that there is the luminosity with all of its appearance yet that luminosity, for the practitioner, is not mistaken, is not stopped off. Stopped luminosity is an experience like luminosity but in which the appearances have, at least to some extent, not been mixed with emptiness.

Vajra Vehicle, Skt. vajrayāna, Tib. rdo rje'i theg pa: See the glossary entry "Great Vehicle".

Wheel of ornamentation of unending enlightened body, speech, and mind, Tib. sku sung thugs mi zad pa'i rgyan gyi 'khor lo: This phrase is used to express final enlightenment as it actually functions. All three vajras of the tathagatas perpetually engage in a limitless expression of enlightenment which is expressed throughout the entirety of the dharmadhatu. It is the single unique sphere of wisdom bursting at the seams with the display of enlightened activity. "Wheel" can be understood to mean "ongoing".

Wisdom, Skt. jñāna, Tib. ye shes: This is a fruition term that refers to the kind of mind—the kind of knower—possessed by a buddha. Sentient beings do have this kind of knower but it is covered over by a very complex apparatus for knowing, that is, dualistic mind. If they practise the path to buddhahood, they will leave behind their obscuration and return to having this kind of knower.

The Sanskrit term has the sense of knowing in the most simple and immediate way. This sort of knowing is present at the core of every being's mind. Therefore, the Tibetans called it "the particular type of awareness which is there primordially". Because of the Tibetan wording it has often been called "primordial wisdom" in English translations, but that goes too far; it is just "wisdom" in the sense of the most fundamental knowing possible.

Wisdom does not operate in the same way as samsaric mind; it comes about in and of itself without depending on cause and effect. Therefore it is frequently referred to as "self-arising wisdom" *q.v.*

About the Author, Padma Karpo Translation Committee, and Their Supports for Study

I have been encouraged over the years by all of my teachers to pass on the knowledge I have accumulated in a lifetime dedicated to study and practice, primarily in the Tibetan tradition of Buddhism. On the one hand, they have encouraged me to teach. On the other, they are concerned that, while many general books on Buddhism have been and are being published, there are few books that present the actual texts of the tradition. Therefore they, together with a number of major figures in the Buddhist book publishing world, have also encouraged me to translate and publish high quality translations of individual texts of the tradition.

My teachers always remark with great appreciation on the extraordinary amount of teaching that I have heard in this life. It allows for highly informed, accurate translations of a sort not usually seen. Briefly, I spent the 1970's studying, practising, then teaching the Gelugpa system at Chenrezig Institute, Australia, where I was a founding member and also the first Australian to be ordained as a monk in the Tibetan Buddhist tradition. In 1980, I moved to the United States to study at the feet of the Vidyadhara Chogyam Trungpa Rinpoche. I stayed in his Vajradhatu community, now called Shambhala, where I studied and practised all the Karma Kagyu, Nyingma, and Shambhala teachings being presented there and was a senior member of the Nalanda Translation Committee. After the vidyadhara's nirvana, I moved in 1992 to Nepal, where I have been continuously involved with the study, practise, translation, and teaching of the Kagyu system and especially of the Nyingma system of Great Completion. In recent years, I have spent extended times in Tibet with the greatest living Tibetan masters of Great Completion, receiving very pure transmissions of the ultimate levels of this teaching directly in Tibetan and practising them there in retreat. In that way, I have studied and practised extensively not in one Tibetan tradition as is usually done, but in three of the four Tibetan traditions—Gelug, Kagyu, and Nyingma—and also in the Theravada tradition, too.

With that as a basis, I have taken a comprehensive and long term approach to the work of translation. For any language, one first must have the lettering needed to write the language. Therefore, as a member of the Nalanda Translation Committee, I spent some years in the 1980's making Tibetan word-processing software and high-quality Tibetan fonts. After that, reliable lexical works are needed. Therefore, during the 1990's I spent some years writing the *Illuminator Tibetan-English Dictionary* and a set of treatises on Tibetan grammar, preparing a variety of key Tibetan reference works needed for the study and translation of Tibetan Buddhist texts, and giving our Tibetan software the tools needed to translate and research Tibetan texts. During this time, I also translated full-time for various Tibetan gurus and ran the Drukpa Kagyu Heritage Project—at the time the largest project in Asia for the preservation of Tibetan Buddhist texts. With the dictionaries, grammar texts, and specialized software in place, and a wealth of knowledge, I turned my attention in the year 2000 to the translation and publication of important texts of Tibetan Buddhist literature.

Padma Karpo Translation Committee (PKTC) was set up to provide a home for the translation and publication work. The committee focusses on producing books containing the best of Tibetan literature, and, especially, books that meet the needs of practitioners. At the time of writing, PKTC has published a wide range of books that, collectively, make a complete program of study for those practising Tibetan Buddhism, and especially for those interested in the higher tantras. All in all, you will find many books both free and for sale on the PKTC web-site. Most are available both as paper editions and e-books.

It would take up too much space here to present an extensive guide to our books and how they can be used as the basis for a study program. However, a guide of that sort is available on the PKTC web-site, whose address is on the copyright page of this book and we recommend that you read it to see how this book fits into the overall scheme of PKTC publications. Other publications from PKTC that explain Great Completion and related matters are:

- *Alchemy of Accomplishment* by Dudjom Rinpoche
- *The Feature of the Expert, Glorious King* by Dza Patrul
- *About the Three Lines* by Dodrupchen III
- *Relics of the Dharmakaya* by Ontrul Tenpay Wangchug
- *Flight of the Garuda* by Zhabkar
- *Peak Doorways to Emancipation* by Shakya Shri
- *Empowerment and AtiYoga* by Tony Duff
- *The Way of the Realized Old Dogs* by Ju Mipham
- *The Method of Preserving the Face of Rigpa* by Ju Mipham
- *Essential Points of Practice* by Shechen Gyaltshab
- *Words of the Old Dog Vijay* by Shechen Gyaltshab
- *Hinting at Dzogchen* by Tony Duff
- *Key Points of Direct Crossing called Nectar of the Pure Part* by Khenchen Padma Namgyal
- *A Presentation of Instructions for the Development Stage Deity "A Stairway Leading To Akanishtha"* by Jigmey Lingpa

We make a point of including, where possible, the relevant Tibetan texts in Tibetan script in our books. We also make them available in electronic editions that can be downloaded free from our web-site, as discussed below. The Tibetan texts for this book are included at the back of the book and are available for download from the PKTC web-site.

Electronic Resources

PKTC has developed a complete range of electronic tools to facilitate the study and translation of Tibetan texts. For many years now, this software has been a prime resource for Tibetan Buddhist centres throughout the world, including in Tibet itself. It is available through the PKTC web-site.

The wordprocessor TibetDoc has the only complete set of tools for creating, correcting, and formatting Tibetan text according to the norms of the Tibetan language. It can also be used to make texts with mixed Tibetan and English or other languages. Extremely high quality Tibetan fonts, based on the forms of Tibetan calligraphy learned from old masters from pre-Communist Chinese Tibet, are also available. Because of their excellence, these typefaces have achieved a legendary status amongst Tibetans.

TibetDoc is used to prepare electronic editions of Tibetan texts in the PKTC text input office in Asia. Tibetan texts are often corrupt so the input texts are carefully corrected prior to distribution. After that, they are made available through the PKTC web-site. These electronic texts are not careless productions like so many of the Tibetan texts found on the web, but are highly reliable editions useful to non-scholars and scholars alike. Some of the larger collections of these texts are for purchase, but most are available for free download.

The electronic texts can be read, searched, and even made into an electronic library using either TibetDoc or our other software, TibetD Reader. Like TibetDoc, TibetD Reader is advanced software with many capabilities made specifically to meet the needs of reading and researching Tibetan texts. PKTC software is for purchase but we make a free version of TibetD Reader available for free download on the PKTC web-site.

A key feature of TibetDoc and Tibet Reader is that Tibetan terms in texts can be looked up on the spot using PKTC's electronic dictionaries. PKTC also has several electronic dictionaries—some Tibetan-Tibetan and some Tibetan-English—and a number of other reference works. The *Illuminator Tibetan-English Dictionary* is renowned for its completeness and accuracy.

This combination of software, texts, reference works, and dictionaries that work together seamlessly has become famous over the years. It has been the basis of many, large publishing projects within the Tibetan Buddhist community around the world for over thirty years and is popular amongst all those needing to work with Tibetan language or deepen their understanding of Buddhism through Tibetan texts.

Tibetan Texts

ཧཱུྃཿ ཀློང་ཆེན་སྙིང་གི་ཐིག་ལེ་ལསཿ གཅོད་ཡུལ་མཁའ་འགྲོའི་གད་རྒྱངས་བཞུགསཿ

ཧཱུྃཿ ཕྱིངས་ཕྱུག་བདེ་ཆེན་མཚོ་རྒྱལ་མ་ལ་ཕྱག་འཚལ་ལོཿ[104] རང་བཞིན་རྫོགས་པ་ཆེན་པོ་ནིཿ ཉག་གཅིག་རྩད་ནས་གཅོད་པའི་ཕྱིརཿ གཅོད་བྱ་གཅོད་བྱེད་ལས་འདས་ཀྱངཿ སྤྲོས་པ་ཅན་གྱི་གང་ཟག་དངཿ བརྟུལ་ཞུགས་སྤྱོད་པ་ལམ་སློང་ཕྱིརཿ ཕུང་པོ་གཟན་བསྐུར་མན་ངག་བསྟནཿ དེ་ལ་མགོ་བའི་ཡོ་བྱད་ནིཿ དྲེགས་པ་ཟིལ་གྱིས་གནོན་པའི་ཕྱིརཿ སྐྱེར་བཞི་

[104] When a revealed treasure break-mark is needed, the Adzom Drukpa edition of the root volumes of Longchen Nyingthig uses the sign shown through out this book ཿ rather than a normal revealed treasure break-mark (༔). However, editions of this text and other texts from the root volumes of Longchen Nyingthig can be found that do use the normal revealed treasure break-marks throughout the text. Those editions must be regarded as suspect because they have been edited by persons without a full knowledge of the tradition.

Note that this sign ཿ looks the same as a visarga of Sanskrit origin but here it is not a visarga but is being used to indicate a revealed treasure mark.

མ་ཉམས་གཅན་གཟན་ལྷགས༔ ལྟ་བ་ཡས་འབུབས་ཅོག་ཕུ[105]་དང༔ སྤྱོད་པ་མས་འཛོགས་
ཁཊྭཾ་ཀ[106]༔ ལྷ་འདྲེ་དབང་སྡུད་མཆོག་ཆེན་རྐང༔ སྣང་བ་ཟིལ་གནོན་ཌཱ་མ་རུ༔ མ་
ཚོགས་དབང་སྒྱུར་དྲིལ་གཡེར་དང༔ སྟག་གཟིག་རས་མ་སྐྲའི་ཅོད་པན༔ མདོར་ན་བརྟུལ་
ཞུགས་སྤྱོད་པ་ལ༔ འོས་པའི་ཆས་རྣམས་སྤྲ་གོན་བྱ༔ དེ་ནས་ས་གནད་གཉན་དམིགས་སུ༔
ཕོ་ཆོད་ལྷ་འདྲེར་བརྙས་སེམས་དང༔ ཆོས་བརྒྱད་བསམ་པས་མ་ཡིན་པར༔ ཚད་མེད་བཞི་
ཡིས་དཔའ་གདེང་བསྐྱེད༔ སྣང་བ་གང་ཤར་ཐོག་བརྡེས་བྱ༔ དེ་ཚེ་ཟིལ་གནོན་དམིགས་པ་
ཡིས༔ མ་གཅུན་དགྲ་ལ་བྱ་ཤོར་མཚུངས༔ དེ་ཕྱིར་རིག་པ་བརྟུལ་ཞུགས་དང༔
ཕཊ༔ཅེས་རང་གི་སྙིང་ག་ནས༔ གནམ་ལྕགས་རྡོ་རྗེ་རྩེ་དགུ་པ༔ སྲ་བརྟན་ལྕི་ཞིང་འཐས་པ་
ལ༔ འོད་ཟེར་མེ་དཔུང་འབར་བ་ཞིག༔ གང་དམིགས་གཉན་སར་ཐོག་ལྟར་ཕོབ༔ དེར་
གནས་ལྷ་འདྲེ་དཔུང་དང་བཅས༔ འབྲོས་ཤིང་འཁྱེར་བའི་དབང་མེད་པར༔ དཔའ་ཟིལ་ཆག་
སྐྱེ་གནས་པར་བསམ༔ དེ་ནས་རྩལ་འཆོས་ངོ་ཚ་སོགས༔ ཐ་མལ་འཁྲུ་འཁྲིགས་བློ་སྤྲངས་
ལ༔ བརྟུལ་ཞུགས་ངར་མའི་གདེང་ལྡན་པས༔ འགྲོ་ལུགས་རྣམ་པ་བཞི་དག་ལས༔ ལྟ་
བའི་གདེང[107] འགྲོས་ཤུགས་ཀྱིས་འགྲོ༔ དེ་ཡང་སྣང་སྲིད་ལྷ་འདྲེ་དང༔ གནས་གདོན་ལམ་
འདྲེ་འཁྲུམ་པོ་ཀུན༔ བཀུག[108] ལར་ལུག་བདས་པ་བཞིན༔ གཉན་སར་རང་དབང་མེད་པར་
གཅུར༔ གནས་དེར་སླེབས་མ་ཐག་ཉིད་དུ༔ དྲག་ཤུལ་འབར་བའི་སྟངས་སྟབས་ཀྱིས༔
ལྷ་འདྲེ་ཀུན་གྱི་རྐང་པ་ནས༔ བཟུང་སྟེ་ཀླད་ལ་ལན་གསུམ་བསྐོར༔ དབང་ཆེན་གཞི་ལ་
བརྡབས་པར་བསམ༔ ཅོག་ཕུ་སྟན་བཅས་ཤུགས་ཀྱིས་བསྒྱུར༔ ལྟ་འདྲེ་ཇི་ལྟར་དབྱིངས་ཆེ་

---

[105] Some editions have ཅོག་བུ་ here and in other places throughout the text instead of the text shown. That is a spelling mistake that comes from Kham dialect.

[106] The spelling shown is incorrect, it should be ཁཊྭཾ་ག་ but all editions have it spelled this way so this is probably the original spelling.

[107] Some copies have གདེངས་ here but that is Kham spelling.

[108] Some copies have བཀུགས་ here but that is Kham spelling.

ཡང་༔ མི་ལྡོངས་མི་སྲིད་ཟླི་ཁོལ་འགྲོ༔ རྣལ་འབྱོར་བརྟུལ་ཞུགས་ཆུང་གྱུར་ན༔ རིམ་པས་ལྷོ་དང་སྦྱར་ཏེ་བྱ༔ དེ་ནས་རང་ཉིད་སྐད་ཅིག་གིས༔ གསང་བ་ཡེ་ཤེས་མཁའ་འགྲོ་མ༔ ཆེ་ཆུང་སྲིད་པའི་གཏོས་དང་མཉམ༔ རྣམ་འགྱུར་རྫོགས་པའི་སྐུར་བསྐྱེད་ལ༔ མི་རྐང་གླིང་བུ་དྲག་ཏུ་འབུད༔ ལྷ་བའི་ངར་བསྐྱེད་བློ་བརྟུང་བྱ༔ ཕཊ༔ འཇིགས་མེད་བརྟུལ་ཞུགས་སྤྱོད་པའི་རྣལ་འབྱོར་ང[109]༔ འཁོར་འདས་མཉམ་པར་བརྡལ་བའི་དགོངས་སྤྱོད་ཀྱིས༔ བདག་འཛིན་ལྷ་འདྲེའི་སྟེང་དུ་བློ་ཞིག་བརྟུང་༔ གཉིས་འཛིན་འཁོར་བའི་རྣམ་རྟོག་རྡུལ་དུ་རློགས༔ རྩ་བརྒྱུད་རིག་འཛིན་བླ་མ་བློ་ལ་བྱོན༔ ཡི་དམ་དཔའ་བོ་རྒྱ་མཚོ་བློ་ལ་བྱོན༔ མཁའ་འགྲོ་གནས་ཉུལ་མ་ཚོགས་བློ་ལ་བྱོན༔ བརྟུལ་ཞུགས་ལམ་དུ་ལོངས་པར་བྱིན་གྱིས་རློབས༔ ཕཊ༔ ཤར་ཕྱོགས་ལུས་འཕགས་གླིང་དུ་བརྟུངས་ཙ་ན༔ དཔའ་བོ་མཁའ་འགྲོའི་བློ་ར་ཟླུམ་ལ་འཁྲིལ༔ ཞི་སྡང་རྒྱལ་པོའི་མགོ་ལ་ཆེམས་སེ་ཆེམ༔ མེ་ལོང་ཡེ་ཤེས་གླིང་བུ་ཀྲུ་རུ་རུ༔ ཧཱུྃ་ཧཱུྃ་ཧཱུྃ༔ ཕཊ༔ ལྷོ་ཡི་འཛམ་བུའི་གླིང་ལ་བརྟུངས་ཙ་ན[110]༔ དཔའ་བོ་མཁའ་འགྲོའི་བློ་ར་ཟླུར་གསུམ་དབལ༔ ང་རྒྱལ་གཤིན་རྗེའི་མགོ་ལ་ཆེམས་སེ་ཆེམ༔ མཉམ་ཉིད་ཡེ་ཤེས་ཐོད་ཐ་ཁྲོ་ལོ་ལོ༔ ཧཱུྃ་ཧཱུྃ་ཧཱུྃ༔ ཕཊ༔ ནུབ་ཀྱི་བ་ལང་སྤྱོད་ལ་བརྟུངས་ཙ་ན༔ དཔའ་བོ་མཁའ་འགྲོའི་བློ་ར་ཟླ་གམ་འཁྲིལ༔ འདོད་ཆགས་སྲིན་མོའི་མགོ་ལ་ཆེམས་སེ་ཆེམ༔ སོར་རྟོག་ཡེ་ཤེས་དྲིལ་གཡེར་ཁྲོ་ལོ་ལོ༔ ཧཱུྃ་ཧཱུྃ་ཧཱུྃ༔ ཕཊ༔ བྱང་གི་སྒྲ་མི་སྙན་ལ་བརྟུངས་ཙ་ན༔ དཔའ་བོ་མཁའ་འགྲོའི་བློ་ར་གྲུ་བཞི་ལམ༔ ཕྲག་དོག་དམ་སྲིའི་མགོ་ལ་ཆེམས་སེ་ཆེམ༔ བྱ་གྲུབ་ཡེ་ཤེས་ཅོད་པན་ཕུ་རུ་རུ༔ ཧཱུྃ་ཧཱུྃ་ཧཱུྃ༔ ཕཊ༔ དབུས་ཕྱོགས་ལྷུན་པོའི་རྩེ་རུ་བརྟུངས་ཙ་ན༔ དཔའ་བོ་མཁའ་འགྲོའི་བློ་ར་ཟླིན་རེ་

[109] Some copies have ངས་ here where the Shechen edition has the text shown. Either could be correct but the author suspects that the Shechen edition is correct.

[110] Some editions have འཛམ་བུ་གླིང་དུ་ but there is no change in meaning.

ཆགས༔ གཏི་མུག་ཤི་འདྲེའི་མགོ་ལ་ཆེམས་སེ་ཆེམ༔ ཆོས་དབྱིངས་ཡེ་ཤེས་ཧཱུྃ་ཀླུ་གྲུ་རུ་རུ༔ ཧཱུྃ་ཧཱུྃ་ཧཱུྃ༔ ཕཊ༔ ཅེས་བརྡུང་ཤེས་པ་གཏད་མེད་བཏང༔ དེ་ནས་ཙོག་པུ་[111] འབུབས་པ་ནི༔ གཞི་དེའི་ལྷ་འདྲེ་གདུག་པ་ཅན༔ གན་རྐྱལ་བསྒྲིལ་བའི་ཡན་ལག་ལྟར༔ གནམ་ལྕགས་ཐུར་བུ་བཏབ་པར་བསམ༔ ཕཊ༔ ཤར་ཕྱོགས་རྡོ་རྗེ་མཁའ་འགྲོ་མས༔ བྱམས་པ་ཆེན་པོའི་ཐུར་པ་ཁྱེར༔ ལྷོ་ཕྱོགས་རིན་ཆེན་མཁའ་འགྲོ་མས༔ སྙིང་རྗེ་ཆེན་པོའི་ཐུར་པ་ཁྱེར༔ ནུབ་ཕྱོགས་པདྨ་མཁའ་འགྲོ་མས༔ དགའ་བ་ཆེན་པོའི་ཐུར་པ་ཁྱེར༔ བྱང་ཕྱོགས་ལས་ཀྱི་མཁའ་འགྲོ་མས༔ བཏང་སྙོམས་ཆེན་པོའི་ཐུར་པ་ཁྱེར༔ དབུས་ཕྱོགས་སངས་རྒྱས་མཁའ་འགྲོ་མས༔ བྱང་ཆུབ་སེམས་ཀྱི་ཐུར་པ་ཁྱེར༔ བདག་འཛིན་ལྷ་འདྲེའི་མགོ་བོ་དང་༔ ལུས་ཚིགས་བཞི་ལ་བཏབ་པ་ཡིས༔ གཡོ་འགུལ་མེད་པར་གནས་པར་གྱུར༔ ཕཊ༔ ཅེས་བརྗོད་བདག་གཞན་ལྷ་འདྲེ་གསུམ༔ གང་དུ་མི་དམིགས་མཉམ་པར་གཞག༔ དེ་ནས་ལྷ་འདྲེ་ངོས་ཟིན་ནས༔ ལུས་སྦྱིན་དངོས་ལ་འཇུག་པ་ནི༔ ཕཊ༔ རང་སྣང་འོད་གསལ་བདེ་བ་ཆེན་པོའི་དབྱིངས༔ འབད་རྩོལ་སྤྲོས་པ་བྲལ་བའི་ནམ་མཁའ་ལ༔ རྩ་བའི་བླ་མ་དྲུག་པ་རྡོ་རྗེ་འཆང་༔ དགོངས་བརྡ་སྙན་བརྒྱུད་བླ་མ་ཡི་དམ་ལྷ༔ མཁའ་འགྲོ་ཆོས་སྐྱོང་སྲུང་མ་སྤྲིན་ལྟར་གཏིབས༔ མ་འགགས་འཇའ་ཚོན་ཐིག་ལེའི་ཀློང་དུ་གསལ༔ ཞེས་པས་ཚོགས་ཞིང་གསལ་བཏབ་ལ༔ ལྷ་འདྲེས་གཙོ་བྱས་སེམས་ཅན་ཀུན༔ ཁྱེད་ཤེས་བློ་ཡིས་སྐྱབས་འགྲོར་དམིགས༔ ཕཊ༔ རང་བྱུང་གི་རིག་པ་བཅོས་མེད་འདི༔ སྐྱབས་ཡུལ་གྱི་ངོ་བོར་མ་རིག་པས༔ སྡུག་བསྔལ་གྱི་རྒྱ་མཚོར་བྱིངས་པ་རྣམས༔ སྐུ་གསུམ་གྱི་དགོངས་པས་བསྐྱབ་ཏུ་གསོལ༔ ལན་གསུམ་དེ་ནས་སེམས་བསྐྱེད་ནི༔ ཕཊ༔ སྣང་བ་ལ་དངོས་པོར་འཛིན་པའི་སེམས༔ བརྟུལ་ཞུགས་ཀྱི་སྤྱོད་པས་ཚར་བཅད་ནས༔ ཡང་དག་གི་གནས་ལུགས་རྟོགས་བྱའི་

[111] As mentioned earlier, some editions have ཙོག་བུ་ which is incorrect.

ཕྱིར༔ རེ་དོགས་དང་བྲལ་བར་སེམས་བསྐྱེད་དོ༔ [112] དེ་ནས་མཎྜལ་ནི༔ ཁོག་པ་རི་རབ༔ ཡན་ལག་གླིང་བཞི༔ ཉིང་ལག་གླིང་ཕྲན༔ མགོ་བོ་ལྷ་གནས༔ མིག་གཉིས་ཉི་ཟླ༔ དོན་སྣོད་ལྷ་མིའི་དཔལ་འབྱོར་དུ་བསམས་ལ༔ ཕཊ༔ གཅེས་འཛིན་གྱི་ཕུང་པོ་སྒྱུ་མའི་ལུས༔ མཎྜལ་གྱི་ཚོམ་བུར་རབ་བཀོད་ནས༔ ཚོགས་ཞིང་གི་ལྷ་ལ་ལྟོས་མེད་འབུལ༔ བདག་འཛིན་གྱི་རྩ་བ་ཆོད་པར་ཤོག༔ ཕཊ༔ དེ་ནས་བླ་མའི་རྣལ་འབྱོར་ནི༔ ཕཊ༔ དབྱིངས་ཟག་མེད་ཆོས་སྐུའི་ནམ་མཁའ་ལ༔ མདངས་འཇའ་ཟེར་ཐིག་ལེར་འཁྲུགས་པའི་དབུས༔ ཕ་དུས་གསུམ་ཀུན་མཁྱེན་པདྨ་འབྱུང་༔ ཚུལ་བརྟུལ་ཞུགས་སྤྱོད་པའི་ཧེ་རུ་ཀ༔ མ་མཁའ་འགྲོ་རྒྱ་མཚོའི་ཚོགས་དང་བཅས༔ སྐུ་མཚན་དཔེའི་གཟི་བྱིན་ཏ་ལ་ལ༔ གསུང་གང་འདུལ་ཆོས་སྒྲ་ཨུ་རུ་རུ༔ ཐུགས་འོད་གསལ་རྡོ་རྗེ་སྙིང་པོའི་ངང་༔ བུ་མོས་གུས་དྲག་པོས་གསོལ་བ་འདེབས༔ ཕྱི་རྣམ་རྟོག་དགྲར་ལངས་ལྷ་འདྲེའི་གཟུགས༔ ནང་རེ་དང་དོགས་པའི་གཉིས་འཛིན་སེམས༔ བར་སྣང་བ་སྣ་ཚོགས་རྐྱེན་ངན་ཀུན༔ ཆོས་ཟབ་མོ་བདུད་ཀྱི་གཅོད་ཡུལ་གྱིས༔ དུས་ད་ལྟ་སྟན་ཐོག་འདི་རུ་ཆོད༔ དབྱིངས་ཆོས་སྐུའི་རྒྱལ་ས་ཟིན་པ་རུ༔ ཕ་རྗེ་བཙུན་བླ་མ་བྱིན་གྱིས་རློབས༔ ཕཊ༔ ཕཊ༔ ཕཊ༔ ཅེས་བརྗོད་ཚོགས་ཞིང་རང་ལ་བསྟིམ༔ གཉིས་མེད་ངང་དུ་མཉམ་པར་གཞག༔ ཕཊ༔ དེ་ནས་བག་ཆགས་སྙིགས་མའི་ལུས༔ ཚོ་ཞིང་སྣུམ་ལ་ལྟོས་ཆེ་བའི༔ དབུས་ལས་དྭངས་མའི་རིག་པ་ནི༔ ཁྲོས་མའི་རྣམ་པར་

[112] One copy here has ཞེས་ལན་གསུམ་ "say this three times" inserted here. That is a personal note that has been entered into someone's copy and is not part of the original text.

པདྨ༔[113] ཅེས་དབྱེ༔ ཞལ་གཅིག་ཕྱག་གཉིས་གྲི་ཐོད་ཅན༔ དེ་ཡིས་རང་ལུས་ཐོད་
པ་ཕྲལ༔ སྟོང་ཁམས་ཁྱབ་པའི་མི་མགོ་ཡི༔ སྒྱེད་བུ་གསུམ་གྱི་ཁར་བཞག
ནང་༔ འབྱུང་ལུས་ཚོགས་སུ་བཤམས་པ་དེ༔ འབྲུ་གསུམ་འོད་ཀྱིས་བདུད་རྩིར་
སྦྱར༔ ཨོཾ་ཨཱཿཧཱུྃ་དང་ཧ་ཧོ་ཧྲཱི[114] ༔ ཅི་མང་བརྗོད་པས་སྦྱངས[115] ་སྤེལ་བསྒྱུར༔ ཁྲ་
བོར་འགྱེད་ན་དེ་ཉིད་ལས༔ སྐྱེད་ཚལ[116] ་ཟས་གོས་སྨན་ལ་སོགས༔ ཡིད་ལ་ཅི་འདོད་ངོ་བོར་
སྤར[117] ་དམར་འགྱེད་རང་ཉིད་ཁྲོས་ནག་མས༔ སྐེགས་མའི་ལུས་ཀྱི་པགས་པ་བཤུས༔ སྟོང་
གསུམ་ཁྱབ་པར་བཀྲམ་པའི་སྟེང་༔ གཟུགས་ཕུང་ཤ་ཁྲག་ཕུང་པོར་སྤུངས༔ ཤན་པའི་
འདུན[118] ་ས་ལྷ་བུར་བསམས༔ ནག་འགྱེད་བདག་གཞན་སེམས་ཅན་གྱི༔ ཐོག་མེད་ནས་
བསགས་ནད་གདོན་དང་༔ སྡིག་སྒྲིབ་ཐམས་ཅད་ནག་བུན་གྱིས༔ བསྡུས་ཏེ་གཟུགས་ཕུང་ལ་

---

[113] Some editions have the visarga removed and replaced with a tsheg. Normally པདྨ should not have a visarga after it but, because of the style of the terma marks used in this text, it is correct to have this mark here and in other places like this later in the text. Some editions have a tsheg after the visarga but that is incorrect too.

[114] Some copies have the དང་ edited out. It must be here otherwise the metre of the poetry, which is correct in all other lines, is broken.

[115] The Shechen edition has སྦྱང་ which is incorrect. It has been corrected as shown.

[116] The Shechen edition is correct as shown, even though most other editions change the wording to སྐྱིད་ཚལ་ or སྐྱེད་ཚུལ་.

[117] Some editions have སྦར་ meaning "to make blaze" but that is incorrect. The text of the Shechen edition is correct as shown.

[118] One copy has མདུན་ but that is incorrect. The text of the Shechen edition is correct as shown.

བསྐྱིམས་པ༔ ལྷ་འདྲེས་ཐོས་བས་ཁོ་ཡི[119]་ལུས༔ སོལ་བ་ལྷ་བུར་སྒྱུར་པར་བསམ༔
མཆོད་སྦྱིན་མགྲོན་རྣམས་འདི་ལྟར་འབོད༔ ཕཊ༔ མཆོད་ཡུལ་རྒྱ་གསུམ་དམ་ཅན་
ནས༔ སྡེ་བརྒྱད་འབྱུང་པོས་གཙོ་བྱས་པའི༔ སྦྱིན་ཡུལ་ལན་ཆགས་འདྲེ་གདོན་
ཡན༔ བརྟུལ་ཞུགས་སྤྱོད་པའི་གནས་འདིར་བྱོན༔ དེ་རིང་འཇིགས་མེད་རྣལ་
འབྱོར་ངས༔ འཁོར་འདས་ཤན་འབྱེད་སྒྱུ་མའི་ལུས༔ སྟོང་གསུམ་ཁྱབ་ཡངས་
ཀ་པཱ་ལར༔ བམ་ཆེན་ཚོགས་ཀྱི་འཁོར་ལོར་བཤམས༔ ཟག་མེད་ཡེ་ཤེས་བདུད་
རྩིར་བསྒྱུར༔ འདོད་དགུར་འཆར་བའི་ཆོ་འཕྲུལ་ཅན༔ གཅེས་འཛིན་མེད་པར་
འབུལ་ལགས་ཀྱིས༔ སྟོན་ཆེན་མགྲོན་ལ་གཤེགས་སུ་གསོལ༔ མཆོག་ཆེན་ཐོད་
ཧ་སྐད་རེ་གསངས༔ ཞིང་ཆེན་གླིང་བུ་གདངས་རེ་སྙན[120]༔ དྲིལ་གཡེར་ཅོད་
པན་དངས་རེ་སྒྲོ༔ བྱ་རྒོད་ཤ་ལ་འཐིབས་པ་བཞིན༔ སྐད་ཅིག་ཉིད་ལ་གཤེགས་
སུ་གསོལ༔ ཕཊ༔ དེ་ནས་འབུལ་ཞིང་བསྔོ་བ་ནི༔ ཕཊ༔ གདོད་མའི་མགོན་
པོ་མན་ཆད་ནས༔ རྩ་བའི་བླ་མ་ཡན་ཆད་ཀྱི༔ བརྒྱུད་གསུམ་རིག་འཛིན་བླ་མ་
དང༔ ཡི་དམ་མཁའ་འགྲོ་ཆོས་སྐྱོང་ལ༔ བམ་ཆེན་བདུད་རྩིའི་མཆོད་པ་
འབུལ༔ ལྷ་འདྲེས་གཙོ་བྱས་བདག་གཞན་གྱིས༔ ཚོགས་གཉིས་རྫོགས་ཤིང་སྒྲིབ་
གཉིས་བྱང༔ བརྟུལ་ཞུགས་འགྲོ་དོན་མཐར་ཕྱིན་ནས༔ སྣང་བ་འོད་གསལ་སྐུ

[119] The Shechen edition has ཁོའི་ but that is incorrect. It has been corrected as shown. There is no change in meaning but the text shown is correct because of a rule of grammar connected with fitting the verse metre.

[120] One edition has this and the previous line replaced with ཞིང་ཆེན་གཡང་གཞི་བརྗིད་རེ་ཆེ༔ མི་རྐང་གླིང་བུ་གདངས་རེ་སྙན༔ meaning "Oh the splendour of the hide of a human with the great grounds! Oh the melody of the human thighbone trumpet so sweet!" Many regard the reading of the Shechen edition, which is shown here, to be correct. Those who follow the other edition with the additional wording, for example, Dzogchen Monastery, regard that wording to be correct.

མར་འབྱོངས༔ ཡང་བག་ཆ་ཆོས་སྐུར་གྲོལ༔ ཧེ་རུ་ཀ་ལྷར་བྱིན་གྱིས་རློབས༔ ཕཊ༔ འཇིག་རྟེན་འདས་དང་མ་འདས་ཀྱིས༔ སྡེ་བརྒྱད་འབྱུང་པོ་མི་མ་ཡིན༔ ལོག་འདྲེན་ཤ་ཟའི་གདོན་ཚོགས་ལ༔ སྟོང་གསུམ་ཁྱབ་པའི་ཞིང་ལྷགས་སྟེང་༔ ཤ་ཁྲག་རུས་པའི་ཕུང་པོར་འབུལ༔ བདག་ཏུ་འཛིན་ན་ང་རེ་ཞེན༔ སྨྱོད་དུ་མ་ནུས་ཁྱོད་རེ་ལོད༔ རིང་ན་རྗེན་པར་ཁྱུར་མིད་ཐོངས༔ ལྷོད་ན་དུམ་བུར་ཆོས་ལ་ཟོ༔ རྡུལ་ཕྲན་ཙམ་ཡང་མ་བཞག་ཅིག༔ ཕཊ༔ འཁོར་ཚེ་ཐོག་མ་མེད་པ་ནས༔ ཤ་འཁོན་ཆགས་པའི་ལན་ཆགས་དང་༔ གློ་བུར་ལྷགས་པའི་སློང་རྗེའི་མགྲོན༔ ཁས་ཞན་དབང་ཆུང་མ་ལུས་ལ༔ སོ་སོ་གང་ལ་ཅི་འདོད་ཀྱིས༔ འདོད་ཡོན་མི་ཟད་གཏེར་དུ་བསྔོ༔ འབྲེལ་བ་ཐོགས་ཚད་སངས་རྒྱས་ཤིང་༔ བུ་ལོན་ལན་ཆགས་བྱང་བར་ཤོག༔ ཕཊ༔ ཅེས་བརྗོད་ལྷོས་པ་མེད་པར་བྱིན༔ སྟོང་ཉིད་ངང་ལ་མཉམ་པར་གཞག༔ དེ་ཚེ་ལུས་ལ་གཅེས་འཛིན་དང་༔ འཇིགས་སྣང་འཁྲུ་འཕྲིགས་བློ་སྐྱེས་ན༔ ལུས་ནི་ལྷ་འདྲེར་བྱིན་ནས་མེད༔ སེམས་ནི་གཞི་མེད་རྩ་བ་བྲལ༔ འདི་བས་སངས་རྒྱས་ཉིད་ཀྱིས་ཀྱང་༔ གཟིགས་པ་མེད་སྙམ་གདེང་བསྐྱེད་ལ༔ གང་ཤར་རང་ངོ་རྩ་གདར་བཅད༔ ཐོགས་བཅས་བདུད་དང་...ཕྱི་རྐྱེན་འབྱུང་བ་དང་གཅན་གཟན་མི་རྒོད་སོགས་དང་ཆགས་སྡང་གི་རྣམ་རྟོག་སོགས། ཐོགས་མེད་བདུད༔...ནང་རྐྱེན་དགའ་སྡུག་སེམས་ཚིག་པ་སོགས། དགའ་བྲོད་བདུད་དང་...རང་མཐོང་བདེ་སྐྱིད་མངོན་རློམ་སོགས། སྙེམས་བྱེད་བདུད༔...ཐེ་ཚོམ་དང་ཁྲུ་འཕྲིགས་ལ་སོགས། ཕཊ༔ཅེས་དབྱིངས་སུ་གཅོད་པ་ཡིན༔ དེ་ཡང་དུས་ཚོད་ལ་མཚོན་ན༔ ཐོ་རངས་ཚོགས་གཉིས་རྫོགས་པའི་ཕྱིར༔ དཀར་འགྲེད་བདུད་རྩིའི་ངོ་བོར་སྒྱུར[121]༔ ཉིན་གུང་ལན་ཆགས་སྦྱོང་བའི་ཕྱིར༔ ཁྲ་འགྲེད་གང་ལ་འཚམས་པར་བསྔོ༔ ནུབ་མོ་བརྟུལ་ཞུགས་ལམ་སློང་ཕྱིར༔ བདག་འཛིན་ཚར་གཅོད་དམར་འགྲེད་གཏོང་༔ སྲོད་ལ་སྡིག་སྦྱོང་ནག་འགྲེད་བྱ༔ ཀུན་ཀྱང་འདུན་པ་བསྒྱུར་བ་སྟེ༔ གཙོ་བོ་དམིགས་པས་ཉམས་སུ་བླང་༔

---

[121] As before, one edition has སྒྲར་ but the Shechen edition is correct as shown. The earlier comments apply.

དེ་ཚེ་ཚོ་འཕྲུལ་ཅི་བྱུང་ཡང་༔ ཉམས་དང་བྲལ་བའི་ལྟ་བས་གཅུན༔ གལ་ཏེ་རྣལ་འབྱོར་དབྱིངས་ཆུད་ནས༔ ལྷོངས་འཚུབས་འཆུན་པར་དཀའ་བའམ༔ ལྷ་འདྲེ་དབྱིངས་ཆེས་མ་ལྷོངས་ན༔ ཀེང་རུས་དཀར་པོའི་དམིགས་པ་བྱ༔ ཕཊ༔ཅེས་རང་ཉིད་སྐད་ཅིག་གིས༔ ཀེང་རུས་དཀར་པོ་མེ་འབར་བ༔ ཤིན་ཏུ་ཆེ་བ[122]་ལས་བྱུང་བའི༔ མེ་ཡིས་སྟོང་གི་འཇིག་རྟེན་དང་༔ ཁྱད་པར་ལྷ་འདྲེའི་གནས་རྟེན་བསྲེགས༔ མཐར་ནི་ཀེང་རུས་མེ་དང་བཅས༔ འོད་ཡལ་སྟོང་པའི་ངང་ལ་གཞག༔ འགོ་ནད་སྲུང་བ་ལ་ཡང་ཟབ༔ ཚར་ཚོད་དུས་སུ་མ་བྱུང་དང་༔ གནོད་འདྲེ་གདུག་པ་ཨར་གཏོད་ན༔ རིག་པ་ཁྲོས་མའི་སྐུར་གསལ་བས༔ སྐྱིགས་མའི་ལུས་ཀྱི་པགས་པ་བཤུས༔ སྟོང་གསུམ་ཁེངས་པའི་གཡང་གཞིའི་སྟེང་༔ ཤ་རུས་གཅལ་དུ་བཀྲམ་པ་ལ༔ འདྲེ་གདོན་ཟས་ལ་གདུང་བའི་མོད༔ ཁྲོས་མས་གཡང་གཞི[123]་ཕུབ་ཀྱིས་དྲིལ༔ སྤྲུལ་དང་རྒྱ་མའི་ཞགས་པས་བསྡམས༔ ཀླད་ལ་བསྣོར་ཞིང་བརྡབས་པ་ཡིས༔ ཤ་སྨུག་རུས་སྨྱུག[124]་དག་ཏུ་སོང་༔ སྤྲུལ་པའི་གཅན་གཟན་དུ་མ་ཡིས༔ ལྷག་མ་མེད་པར་ཟོས་པར་བསམ༔ དབྱིངས་རིག་བསྲེས་ཏེ་མཉམ་པར་གཞག༔ དེས་ནི་ཚར་ཚོད་ངེས་འབྱུང་ཞིང་༔ འདྲེ་གདོན་གདུག་པ་ཚར་ཆོད་འགྱུར༔ ཀུན་ལ་གཅེས་འཛིན་བློ་སྦྱངས་ཏེ༔ ལྟ་བའི་གདེང་གིས་ཟིན་པ་གཅེས༔ དེ་ཚེ་ཚར་ཚོད་འདྲ་བའི་ལྷོངས༔ ལྷོངས་ཚོད་འདྲ་བའི་ཚར་ཚོད་དང་༔ གཉིས་ཀ་འདྲ་བའི་འདྲེས་མ་དང་༔ འདྲེས་མ་འདྲ་བའི་བག་ཆགས་དང་༔ ཚར་ལྷོངས་གཉིས་ཀ་མཐར་ཕྱིན་གྱི༔ རྟགས་རྣམས་ཉམས་དང་སྦྱར་ཏེ་སྦྱད༔ དོན་ལ་བདག་མེད་ཀུན་བཟང་མོ༔ ཡུམ་ཆེན་ཤེས་རབ་ཕར་ཕྱིན་མའི༔ དགོངས་པ་ཀློང་དུ་གྱུར་ཙ་ན༔

[122] The Shechen edition is indistinct here and looks as though the print plate has been retouched. It has been corrected as shown. Some copies change it to ཚ་པོ་ which is incorrect.

[123] The Shechen edition here has བཞི་ which is incorrect. It has been corrected as shown.

[124] One edition has ཤ་སྨུག་རུས་སྨྱུག་ but that is impossible. The Shechen edition has the spelling as shown, which is a play on the term སྨུག་སྨྱུག་.

གཅོད་ཡུལ་ལམ་དུ་ཡོངས་པའོ༔ ས་མ་ཡ༔ རྗེས་ལ་བསྔོ་སྨོན་བྱ་བ་ནི༔ ཨཱ༔ དགེ་དང་མི་དགེའི་རྟོག་ཚོགས་རང་གྲོལ་ལ༔ རེ་དང་དོགས་པའི་མཚན་མ་མི་དམིགས་ཀྱང་༔ སྣང་ཆའི་རྟེན་འབྲེལ་བསླུ་མེད་དགེ་ཚོགས་རྒྱུན༔ ཟག་མེད་ཆོས་ཀྱི་དབྱིངས་སུ་བསྔོ་བར་བྱ༔ ཕཊ༔ ཀུན་རྫོབ་ལུས་ཀྱི་སྦྱིན་པ་ལ་བརྟེན་ནས༔ བསྐལ་པར་[125] བསགས་པའི་བུ་ལོན་ལན་ཆགས་བྱང་༔ དོན་དམ་ཆོས་ཀྱི་བདེན་པས་རྒྱུད་འགྲོལ་ཚེ༔ བདག་གི་འདུས་པ་དང་པོར་སྐྱེ་བར་ཤོག༔ དེ་ཚེ་མ་བཅོས་རང་བཞག་གཉུག་མའི་དོན༔ མི་བསྒྱུར་ལྷ་འདྲེའི་རྒྱུད་ལ་སྐྱེས་ནས་ཀྱང་༔ ངར་འཛིན་འཁྲུལ་པའི་རྗེས་སུ་མི་འབྲང[126] བར༔ བྱམས་དང་སྙིང་རྗེས་ཤེས་རྒྱུད་བརླན་པར་ཤོག༔ བདག་ཀྱང་བརྟུལ་ཞུགས་སྤྱོད་པ་མཐར་ཕྱིན་ནས༔ སྲིད་སྡུག་རོ་སྙོམས་འཁོར་འདས་ཆོས་སྐུར་འབྱོངས༔ ཕྱོགས་ལས་རྣམ་རྒྱལ་འབྲེལ་ཚད་དོན་ལྡན་གྱིས༔ ཕྲིན་ལས་མཐར་ཕྱིན་འཇའ་ལུས་འགྲུབ་པར་ཤོག༔ ཕཊ༔ ཅེས་བརྗོད་ལྟ་བའི་ངང་མདངས་བསྐྱངས༔ སྙིང་རྗེ་ཆེན་པོའི་རྩིས་ཟིན་པས༔ བདེ་སྡུག་...བདག་གི་བདེ་བ་ལྷ་འདྲེར་གཏོང་། ལྷ་འདྲེའི་སྡུག་བསྔལ་རང་གིས་བླ། གཏོང་ལེན་དམིགས་པ་དང་༔ ཆོས་ཀྱི་སྦྱིན་པ་...ཆོས་རྣམས་ཐམས་ཅད་རྒྱུ་ལས་བྱུང་། སོགས་དང་། སྡིག་པ་ཅི་ཡང་མི་བྱ་ཞིང་། སོགས་དང་། འབྱུང་པོ་གང་དག་སོགས་ཀྱི་ཤིས་བརྗོད་བྱའོ། རྣམ་དག་བྱ༔ འབྲེལ་ཐོགས་བཟང་ངན་ཐར་ལམ་འགོད༔ ས་མ་ཡ[127] ༔ མ་མ་ཀོ་ལིང་ས་མནྟ༔

[125] One edition has རང་གཞན་ here instead of the text shown but that is a mistake. The prayer is well-known and has its wording as shown.

[126] One edition has འབྱེངས་ instead of the text shown. This is another example of a re-spelling of the original using a form common in Kham.

[127] One edition has ས་མྺ་ཡ་ samaya which is a more correct spelling of the Sanskrit involved. However, after some research, it looks as though the original edition did have the spelling shown.

ཨོཾ་ སྙན་ལ་རིང་བ་བུང་བའི་སྐད་ལྟ་བུ། ཧཱུྃ་ ཇམས་ལ་འཚོར་བ་ཧྲ་སྐད་ལྟ་བུ། ཏྲཱྃ་
དྲག་ལ་གཏུམ་པ་སྟག་མོའི་ངར་སྐད་ལྟ་བུ། ཧྲཱིཿ འགྱུར་ལ་ལྷེམ་པ་དྲི་ཟའི་སྐད་ལྟ་བུ།
ཨཱཿ འགྱུར་ལྷེམ་གོང་འདྲ་ནས་གཞམ་འདེགས་ཙམ་བྱེད་པ་ལ་ཌཱ་ཀིའི་སྒྲུག་སྒྲུ་ཟེར།།

༄༅། །གཅོད་ཡུལ་མཁའ་འགྲོའི་གད་རྒྱངས་ཀྱི་མན་ངག་ཟབ་མོ་བཞུགས་སོ།།

༄༅། །རྡོ་རྗེ་རྣོན་པོ་རལ་གྲི་ཆེ། །ཡི་གེ་མཆོག་སྟེ་རྣམ་པར་དག །ཐེག་པ་ཆེན་པོ་སྡུག་བསྔལ་གཅོད། །མཚོན་ཆ་ཆེན་པོ་ཕཊ༔ལ་འདུད། །ཕ་རོལ་ཕྱིན་པ་ཀུན་རྫོགས་པ། །ས་རྣམས་ཀུན་གྱི་རྒྱན་དང་ལྡན། །རྣམ་པར་དག་པ་བདག་མེད་ཆོས། །ཟབ་དོན་གཅོད་ཀྱི་ཉམས་ལེན་བྲི། །དེ་ལ་ཟབ་དོན་གྱི་གདམས་པ་ཉམས་སུ་ལེན་པའི་སྐབས་སུ་སྔོན་འགྲོའི་སྦྱངས་པ་རྣམས་དང་། དངོས་གཞི་ཡུམ་དོན་ངོ་སྤྲོད་པ། བདུད་བཞི་དབྱིངས་སུ་གཅོད་པ་སོགས་ཉམས་ལེན་གནད་དུ་ཁེལ་ཞིང་། རྗེས་ཐོབ་འདོན་སྤྱོད་པས་ལ་བརླ་བའི་ཆེད་དུ་གཉན་སར་འགྲོ་བའི་ཚེ། ཟིལ་གནོན་དམིགས་པ་སྐོར་གསུམ་དང་། ཉམས་ལེན་ཕུང་པོ་ཟན་བསྒྱུར་རྣམས་གཅོད་ཡུལ་མཁའ་འགྲོའི་གད་རྒྱངས་ལྟར་བྱ་བ་ལ། དང་པོ་སྟ་གནོན་གྱི་དམིགས་པ་ནི། ཕཊ༔ཅེས་བརྗོད་པས་རང་གི་ཐུགས་ཀ་ནས་གནམ་ལྕགས་ཀྱི་རྡོ་རྗེ་རྩེ་དགུ་པ་སྦྲ་ཞིང་བརྟན་པ། ལྕི་ཞིང་འཐས་པ་འོད་ཟེར་དང་མེ་དཔུང་གི་ཚྭ་ཚྭ་འཕྲོ་བ་ཞིག་གང་དམིགས་པའི་གཉན་ས་འདིར་དཔག་ཆེན་གྱིས་མདའ་འཕངས་པ་ལྟར་སོང་སྟེ་གནམ་ལྕགས་ཀྱི་ཐོག་ལྷུང་བ་ལྟར་བབས་ནས་འོད་དང་འོད་ཟེར་དུ་འཕྲོ་ཞིང་མེ་དཔུང་གི་ཚྭ་ཚྭ་ཐོ་རོ་རོ་འཕྲོས་པས་ས་དེ་ན་གནས་པའི་ལྷ་འདྲེ་སྡེ་དང་དཔུང་དུ་བཅས་པ་ཐམས་ཅད་འཕྲོས་ཤིང་འཁྱར་བའི་དབང་མེད་པར་དཔའ་ཟིལ་ང་རྒྱལ་ཆག །སྙེམས་པའི་སྣང་ཤོར་ནས་ཟིལ་ཆུམ་གྱིས་གནས་པར་བསམ། དེ་ནས་འགྲོ་བའི་ཚེ། ཕོ་ཆོད་ལྷ་འདྲེར་བརླས་སེམས་དང་། ཆོས་བརྒྱུད་བསམ་པས་ཡིན་པར། །ཞེས་པ་ལྟར། བདག་མེད་གནས་ལུགས་རྟོགས་པའི་ལྟ་བའི་གདིང་དང་། འབྲེལ་ཚད་ཐར་ལམ་ལ་འགོད་པའི་ལྷ་འདྲེའི་འགྲོ་དོན་བྱེད་སྙམ་པའི་སྙིང་རྗེ་བྱང་ཆུབ་སེམས་ཀྱི་ལུགས་དང་ལྡན་པས་འགྲོ། གཉན་སར་ཕྱིན་ནས། བར་གནོན་གྱི་དམིགས་པ་ནི། ཕཊ༔ཅེས་བརྗོད་པས་རང་ཉིད་སྐད་ཅིག་གིས་གསང་བ་ཡེ་ཤེས་ཀྱི་མཁའ་འགྲོ་བདེ་ཆེན་རྡོ་རྗེ

རྣལ་འབྱོར་མ། ཐུགས་སྙིང་རྗེ་ཆེན་པོས་སེམས་ཅན་ལ་རྗེས་སུ་ཆགས་ཤིང་། ཁམས་གསུམ་དབང་དུ་སྡུད་པའི་བརྡར་སྐུ་མདོག་དམར་མོ་དུས་མཐའི་མེའི་འོད་ཟེར་ལྟར་འབར་བ། ཐུགས་བདེ་བ་ཆེན་པོའི་ཡེ་ཤེས་ཀྱི་ཀློང་དུ་དུག་གསུམ་དབྱིངས་སུ་དག་ཅིང་སྲིད་གསུམ་ཟིལ་གྱིས་གནོན་པའི་བརྡར་ཉི་མ་འབུམ་ལྟར་གཟི་བརྗིད་འབར་ཞིང་ཁྲོ་བའི་ཉམས་དང་ལྡན་པ། ཆོས་ཐྲ་ཡིད་ཀྱི་བག་ཆགས་དབྱིངས་སུ་དག་ཅིང་། ཐུགས་མི་ཟད་པ་རྒྱན་གྱི་འཁོར་ལོ་ལ་མངའ་དབང་འབྱོར་པས་སྐུ་སྟོད་གཟུགས་མེད་སྲིད་པའི་རྩེ་ན་བརྗིད་པ། ཐྲ་བདག་གི་བག་ཆགས་དབྱིངས་སུ་དག་ཅིང་གསུང་མི་ཟད་རྒྱན་གྱི་འཁོར་ལོ་ལ་མངའ་དབང་འབྱོར་བས་སྐུ་སྐེད་གཟུགས་ཀྱི་ཁམས་ན་འཕྲིང་བ། རགས་པ་ལུས་ཀྱི་བག་ཆགས་དབྱིངས་སུ་དག་ཅིང་སྐུ་མི་ཟད་བརྒྱན་གྱི་འཁོར་ལོ་ལ་མངའ་དབང་འབྱོར་བས་སྐུ་སྨད་འདོད་ཁམས་ཀྱི་གནས་སུ་རོལ་བ། བདེ་ཆེན་སྒྱུ་མའི་གང་གིས་སྲིད་གསུམ་ཕྱག་རྒྱས་འགོངས་བའི་རྡོ་རྗེའི་གར་སྟབས་བསྒྱུར་བ། འགྱུར་མེད་ཆོས་སྐུའི་ཀློང་དུ་འཁོར་འདས་ཐིག་ལེ་ཉག་གཅིག་ཏུ་རྫོགས་པས་ཞལ་གཅིག་པ། ཤེས་པས་སྲིད་ལ་མི་གནས་ཤིང་། སྲིད་མཐའི་འཁྲུལ་པ་གཅོད་པའི་བརྡར་གནག་སྐུམ་དབུ་སྐྲའི་ཐོར་ཅོག་བཅིངས་པ། སྙིང་རྗེས་ཞི་མཐར་མི་གནས་ཤིང་ཞི་མཐར་ཞེན་པ་དགག་པའི་བརྡར་རལ་པའི་ཟུར་ཕུད་ཐུར་དུ་འཕྱང་བས་སྐུ་རྒྱབ་ཁེབ་པ། སྐུ་གསུམ་ལྷུན་གྱིས་གྲུབ་ཅིང་ཐུགས་རྗེས་འགྲོ་ལ་གཟིགས་པའི་ཕྱིར་དམར་ལ་ཟླུམ་པའི་སྤྱན་གསུམ་རྒྱས་པ། ཚད་མེད་རྣམ་བཞིས་འགྲོ་དོན་མཛད་ཅིང་རྣམ་པ་བཞིའི་ལས་རྒྱུན་མི་ཆད་པའི་ཕྱིར་མཆེ་བ་བཞི་རྣོ་ངར་དུ་གཙིགས་པ། ཚངས་པའི་དབྱངས་ཀྱི་ཡན་ལག་རྫོགས་ཤིང་འཁྲུལ་སྣང་གདོན་གྱི་མགོ་བོ་འགེམས་པས་གློག་དམར་ལྟ་བུའི་ལྗགས་བཀྲུངས་ཤིང་ཕཊ་དང་ཕེམ་སྒྲ་སྒྲོག་པ། ཐབས་དང་ཤེས་རབ་འདུ་འབྲལ་མེད་ཅིང་ཟུང་འཇུག་རྡོ་རྗེའི་ལམ་གྱིས་འཁོར་འདས་དབྱེར་མེད་དུ་སྒྱུར་བའི་ཕྱིར་ཕྱག་གཉིས་པ། སྙིང་རྗེ་ཆེན་པོས་ཀླན་ཞིང་བསྐུ་བཞིའི་ཕྲིན་ལས་རྫོགས་པའི་བརྡར་ཕྱག་གཡས་ཁྲག་གིས་གོས་པའི་མི་ལྤགས་ཀྱི་གཡང་གཞི་དམར་ལྷབ་ལྷབ་ཏུ་བརྟེབས་པས་ལྷ་འདྲེ་མི་གསུམ་དབང་དུ་སྡུད་ཅིང་བྲན་དུ་བཀོལ་བར་བྱེད་པ། ཞེས་

རབ་སྟོང་ཉིད་ཆོས་ཀྱི་རང་སྒྲས་སྒྲེ་རྒྱུའི་མ་རིག་གཉིད་ལས་སློང་བའི་བརྡར་ཕྱག་གཡོན་
མི་རྐང་གི་གླིང་བུ་དྲག་ཏུ་འབུད་པས་འཇིག་རྟེན་གྱི་དྲེགས་བྱེད་ཟིལ་གྱིས་གནོན་ཅིང་ང་
རྒྱལ་འཛོམས་པ། དུག་ལྔ་ལམ་དུ་བྱེད་ཅིང་ཕུང་པོ་ལྔ་དབྱིངས་སུ་དག་སྟེ་སྐུ་ལྔས་
འགྲོ་དོན་མཛད་ལ་རིགས་ལྔའི་དབང་བསྐུར་རྫོགས་པས་ཐོད་པ་སྐམ་པོ་ལྔས་དབུ་བརྒྱན་
པ། ཤེས་རབ་ཡུམ་གྱི་སྐུ་ལ་ཐབས་ཆེན་སྤྱོད་པའི་ཕྱོགས་ཀྱི་ཕ་རོལ་ཕྱིན་པ་ལྔ་འདུ་
འབྲལ་མེད་པའི་བརྡར་རྡུས་པའི་ཕྱག་རྒྱ་ལྔས་བརྒྱན་པ། ཀློང་དགུའི་དབྱིངས་ལ་
རོལ་ཞིང་ས་དགུའི་བག་ཆགས་དག་ནས་ཀུན་སྦྱོར་འཆིང་བ་གཅོད་པས་གར་དགུའི་
ཉམས་ཀྱིས་སྒེག་པ། ཚོགས་གཉིས་ཟུང་དུ་འཇུག་ཅིང་སྲིད་ཞིའི་ཡུལ་ལས་འདས་པ་
དོན་གཉིས་ལྷུན་གྱིས་གྲུབ་པའི་ཕྱིར་ཞབས་གཉིས་གར་སྟབས་ཀྱིས་རོལ་བའོ། །དེའི་
སྟེང་གི་ནམ་མཁར་གཅོད་ཡུལ་བརྒྱུད་པའི་བླ་མ་ཐམས་ཅད་སྐུ་རྡོ་རྗེའི་གར་སྟབས་
བསྒྱུར་བ། གསུང་ཚངས་དབྱངས་ཀྱི་མགུར་གླུ་སྒྲོག་པ། ཐུགས་བདེ་ཆེན་གྱི་
ཉམས་སྣང་འུར་བ། འཇའ་དང་འོད་ཕུང་གི་ཀློང་ན་བྱིན་འཐིབས་སེ། འོད་
སྤྲུངས་སེ། བག་དྲོ་ཆིལ་ལེར་བཞུགས་པ། བར་གྱི་ནམ་མཁའ་ལ་ཡི་དམ་རྒྱུད་
སྡེ་བཞི་དྲུག་གི་ལྷ་ཚོགས་མེ་རི་མེ་དཔུང་འཇའ་དང་འོད་ཕུང་གི་ཀློང་ན་སྐུ་སྣ་ཚོགས་ཀྱི་
ཕྱག་རྒྱ་བསྒྱུར་བ། གསུང་དགྱེས་པའི་གད་མོ་སྒྲོག་པ། ཐུགས་སྙིང་རྗེ་ཆེན་པོའི་
དགོངས་པ་ལ་རོལ་བ། ཞི་བ་རྣམས་ཚུལ་དགུའི་ཉམས་ཀྱིས་སྒེག་ཅིང༌། ཁྲོ་བོ་
རྣམས་གར་དགུའི་སྟབས་ཀྱིས་རོལ་བ། རང་གི་འཁོར་དུ་གནས་ཡུལ་དུར་ཁྲོད་ཀྱི་
ཞིང་སྐྱོང་གི་མཁའ་འགྲོ། དཀར་མོ་མཛེས་འཛུམ་སྐྱུའི་ཌཱ་ཀི་འབུམ་སྡེ། དམར་
མོ་རྗེས་ཆགས་གསུང་གི་ཌཱ་ཀི་འབུམ་སྡེ། སྔོན་མོ་གར་བསྒྱུར་ཐུགས་ཀྱི་ཌཱ་ཀི་
འབུམ་སྡེ། སེར་མོ་སྣག་འཆང་ཡོན་ཏན་གྱི་ཌཱ་ཀི་འབུམ་སྡེ། ལྗང་མོ་ཁྲོ་གཏུམ་
ཕྲིན་ལས་ཀྱི་ཌཱ་ཀི་འབུམ་སྡེ། ཐམས་ཅད་ཀྱང་ལ་ལ་གཞོན་ཉམས་ལང་ཚོས་སྒེག
ཅིང༌། གནག་སྣུམ་དབུ་སྐྲའི་ཟར་བུ་གཡོ་བ་ཐོར་ཚུགས་རུས་རྒྱན་དྲིལ་གཡེར་
འཁྲོལ་ཞིང་སྣ་ཚོགས་དར་གྱི་ཅོད་པན་འཕྱུར་བ། ལ་ལ་བགྲེས་ཉམས་གཟི་བརྗིད་
རྗམས་ཤིང་དབུ་སྐྲ་སེར་པོ་ལྷག་པར་བཅིངས་པ། སྐུམ་དང་ཁྲག་གི་ཐིག་ལེས་བརྒྱན་

ཅིང་རོ་ཆས་སྙིང་པའི་ན་བཟའ་གསོལ་བ། ཁ་ན་སོ་མེད་ཏ་ཏ་ཐོད་ཅིང་རྐང་པ་གར་སྟབས་འཁྲོལ་ཞིང་འགྲོ་བ། ལ་ལ་ཞི་བའི་འཛུམ་མདངས་གསལ་བ། ལ་ལ་ཁྲོ་བའི་གར་དགུ་རོལ་པ། ལ་ལ་ཞི་ཁྲོ་སྤྱིད་མའི་ཉམས་ཅན། རྣམ་རྟོག་དབྱིངས་སུ་གསོད་པས་ལ་ལ་གསོད་བྱེད་ཀྱི་ཤན་པ་ལྟར་སྟོན་པ། བག་ཆགས་ཀྱི་དྲི་མ་འབྲུད་པས་ལ་ལ་དག་བྱེད་ཀྱི་ཁྲུས་མཁན་ལྟར་སྟོན་པ། ཉོན་མོངས་ཡེ་ཤེས་སུ་བསྒྱུར་བས་ལ་ལ་སྒྱུར་བྱེད་ཚོས་མཁན་ལྟར་སྟོན་པ། ཏིང་འཛིན་ཉམས་ཀྱིས་འཚོ་བས་ལ་ལ་འཚོ་བྱེད་གཡོས་མཁན་ལྟར་སྟོན་པ། འགྲོ་དྲུག་རྗེས་སུ་འཛིན་པས་ལ་ལ་སླུ་བྱེད་གཡེམ་མཁན་ལྟར་སྟོན་པ། དེ་དག་ཐམས་ཅད་ཀྱང་རིག་སྟོང་ལྟ་བའི་ཀློང་དུ་ཆོས་སྐུ་དབྱིངས་ཀྱི་མཁའ་འགྲོ་རྫོགས་པ། འཛིན་མེད་སྒོམ་པའི་ཀློང་དུ་ལོངས་སྐུ་ཡེ་ཤེས་ཀྱི་མཁའ་འགྲོ་བཞུགས་པ། ཞེན་མེད་སྤྱོད་པའི་ཀློང་དུ་སྤྲུལ་སྐུ་ལས་ཀྱི་མཁའ་འགྲོ་ལྟར་སྟོན་པ། ཆགས་མེད་འབྲས་བུ་རྫོགས་པའི་ཤ་ཟ་འཇིག་རྟེན་གྱི་མཁའ་འགྲོ་ཐམས་ཅད་བྲན་དུ་ཁོལ་བ། དེ་དག་གི་མཁའ་བསྐོར་དུ་ཡེ་ཤེས་དང་ལས་ལས་གྲུབ་པའི་ཆོས་སྐྱོང་སྲུང་མ་ཐམས་ཅད་སྐུ་མདོག་དང་ཞལ་ཕྱག་གི་རྣམ་འགྱུར་མ་ངེས་ཤིང་། ཞི་ཁྲོའི་ཉམས་སྣ་ཚོགས་སུ་གསལ་བ། ཐམས་ཅད་ཀྱང་སྐུ་བྲོ་དང་གར་གྱི་རྣམ་འགྱུར་རོམས་ཤིང་། གསུང་ཧཱུྃ་གི་གླུ་དང་ཕཊཿཀྱི་སྒྲ་སྒྲོག་པ། དེ་ལྟར་གཙོ་དང་འཁོར་དུ་བཅས་པ་ཐམས་ཅད་ཀྱང་ཐུགས་བརྟུལ་ཞུགས་སྤྱོད་པའི་ཉམས་དང་ལྡན་པའི་སྒོ་ནས་འཁོར་འདས་དབྱེར་མེད་བརྡལ་ཞིང་གཉིས་འཛིན་འཁོར་བའི་རྣམ་རྟོག་གཞོམ་པའི་ཆེད་དུ། ཤར་ཕྱོགས་བྱམས་པ་ཆེན་པོའི་རང་བཞིན་འཇའ་འོད་དཀར་གསལ་གྱི་གྲོ་ར་ལུས་འཕགས་གླིང་གི་རྣམ་པར་གནས་པའི་དབུས་སུ་ཞེ་སྡང་ཁྲོ་གཏུམ་གྱི་རྟོག་པ་ཐམས་ཅད་ཕོ་གདོན་རྒྱལ་པོའི་རྣམ་པར་ཁ་སྦྲུབས་སུ་བསྒྲིལ་བའི་སྟེང་དུ་ཞི་བའི་གྲོ་ར་ཟླུམ་འཁྱིལ་དུ་བཅས་ནས་གྲོ་བརྡུངས་པས་ཞེ་སྡང་མེ་ལོང་ཡེ་ཤེས་སུ་དག་སྟེ། རིག་རྩལ་བྱམས་པ་ཆེན་པོའི་ཏིང་འཛིན་དུ་ཤར། ལྷོ་ཕྱོགས་སྙིང་རྗེ་ཆེན་པོའི་རང་བཞིན་འཇའ་འོད་མཐིང་གསལ་གྱི་གྲོ་ར་འཛམ་བུའི་གླིང་གི་རྣམ་པར་གནས་པའི་དབུས་སུ་ང་རྒྱལ་ཁེངས་དྲེགས་ཀྱི་རྟོག་པ་ཐམས་ཅད་གསོད་བྱེད་གཤིན་རྗེའི་གདོན་ཚོགས་ཀྱི་རྣམ་

པར་ཁ་སྦྱུབས་སུ་བསྐྱིལ་བའི་སྟེང་དུ་རྒྱས་པའི་བྲོ་ར་གྲུ་བཞིར་བཅས་ནས་བྲོ་བརྡུངས་པས་ང་རྒྱལ་མཉམ་ཉིད་ཡེ་ཤེས་སུ་དག་སྟེ། རིག་རྩལ་སྙིང་རྗེ་ཆེན་པོའི་རྣམ་པར་ཤར། ནུབ་ཕྱོགས་དགའ་བ་ཆེན་པོའི་རང་བཞིན་འཇའ་འོད་དམར་གསལ་གྱི་བྲོ་ར་བ་ལང་སྤྱོད་ཀྱི་རྣམ་པར་གནས་པའི་དབུས་སུ་འདོད་ཆགས་ཞེན་པའི་རྟོག་པ་ཐམས་ཅད་མོ་གདོན་སྲིན་མོའི་རྣམ་པར་གན་རྐྱལ་དུ་བསྐྱིལ་བའི་སྟེང་དུ་དབང་གི་བྲོ་ར་ཟླ་གམ་དུ་བཅས་ནས་བྲོ་བརྡུངས་པས་འདོད་ཆགས་སོར་རྟོག་ཡེ་ཤེས་སུ་དག་སྟེ། རིག་རྩལ་དགའ་བ་ཆེན་པོའི་ཏིང་འཛིན་དུ་ཤར། བྱང་ཕྱོགས་བཏང་སྙོམས་ཆེན་པོའི་རང་བཞིན་འཇའ་འོད་སེར་གསལ་གྱི་བྲོ་ར་སྦྲ་མི་སྣན་གྱི་རྣམ་པར་གནས་པའི་དབུས་སུ་ཕྲག་དོག་གདུག་པའི་རྟོག་པ་ཐམས་ཅད་སླུ་བྱེད་དམ་སྲིའི་གདོན་གྱི་རྣམ་པར་གན་རྐྱལ་དུ་བསྐྱིལ་བའི་སྟེང་དུ་དྲག་པོའི་བྲོ་ར་གྲུ་གསུམ་དུ་བཅས་ནས་བྲོ་བརྡུངས་པས་ཕྲག་དོག་བྱ་གྲུབ་ཡེ་ཤེས་སུ་དག་སྟེ། རིག་རྩལ་བཏང་སྙོམས་ཆེན་པོའི་ཏིང་འཛིན་དུ་ཤར། དབུས་ཕྱོགས་བྱང་ཆུབ་སེམས་ཀྱི་རང་བཞིན་གྱི་བྲོ་ར་གཞི་ཚད་མེད་བཞིའི་རང་འོད་གསལ་ཞིང་བསྡུ་དངོས་བཞིའི་བང་རིམ་བཀྲ་ལ་ཕར་ཕྱིན་དྲུག་གི་ཁ་ཁྱེར་ཡངས་པའི་རི་རྒྱལ་ལྷུན་པོའི་རྣམ་པར་གནས་པའི་སྟེང་དུ་གཏི་མུག་རྨོངས་པས་བསྐྱེད་པའི་ཀུན་རྟོག་འཁྲུལ་པའི་སྣང་བ་ཅི་སྙེད་ཅིག་ཡོད་པ་ཐམས་ཅད་ཤི་འདྲེ་གསོན་འདྲེ་ཡུལ་འདྲེ་འཁྲུམས་པོ་གནས་གདོན་ལུས་གདོན་སོགས་སྣང་སྲིད་ལྷ་འདྲེའི་རྣམ་པར་གཅལ་དུ་བཀྲམ་པའི་སྟེང་དུ་ཆོས་ཀྱི་དབྱིངས་ཀྱི་བྲོ་ར་བྱིན་ཆགས་པ་བཅས་ནས་བྲོ་བརྡུངས་པས་གཏི་མུག་ཆོས་དབྱིངས་ཡེ་ཤེས་སུ་དག་སྟེ། རིག་རྩལ་བྱང་ཆུབ་སེམས་སུ་འབར་བས་སྟོང་ཉིད་སྙིང་རྗེ་ཟུང་དུ་འབྲེལ་ཏེ། འཁོར་བ་མྱུར་འདས་སུ་དག་སྟེ་རེ་དོགས་སྤང་བླང་གི་རྣམ་རྟོག་ཐམས་ཅད་དབྱིངས་སུ་དག་པར་བསམ་ཞིང་བྲོ་བརྡུང་བར་བྱའོ། །དེ་ནས་སླར་ཡང་རང་གི་ཐུགས་ཀ་ནས་འཕྲོས་པའི་འོད་ཟེར་དང་ལས་བྱེད་མཁའ་འགྲོ་མ་གྲངས་མེད་པ་རྣམས་ཀྱིས་འཁྲུལ་གཟུགས་གདོན་གྱི་རྣམ་པར་ཤར་བའི་སྣང་ཞིང་སྲིད་པའི་ལྷ་འདྲེ་ཐམས་ཅད་དང་། ཁྱད་པར་ཡུལ་ཕྱོགས་འདི་ན་གནས་པའི་ལྷ་འདྲེ་གདུག་པ་ཅན་གང་ཡིན་པ་དེ་རང་དབང་མེད་པར་བཀུག་ནས་གན་རྐྱལ་དུ་བསྐྱིལ་བའི་ཡན་ལག་ལྟར་

ཕུར་པ་འདེབས་པ་སྟེ། དེ་ཡང་རང་རིག་ཆོས་དབྱིངས་ཡེ་ཤེས་ཀྱི་རང་གདངས་རྡོ་རྗེ་རིགས་ཀྱི་མཁའ་འགྲོ་དཀར་མོ་ཞི་འཛུམ་མཛེས་པའི་ཉམས་དང་ལྡན་པས་རིག་རྩལ་བྱམས་པ་ཆེན་པོའི་རང་བཞིན་ཞི་བའི་ཕུར་པ་དཀར་པོ་ཟླུམ་པོའི་རྣམ་པ་ཅན་བདག་འཛིན་ལྷ་འདྲེའི་གཟུགས་ཀྱི་ལག་གཡས་ཞེ་སྡང་གི་རང་བཞིན་ལ་བཏབ་པས་ཞེ་སྡང་གནོད་སེམས་ཀྱི་རྟོག་པ་སྐད་ཅིག་ཀྱང་མི་གཡོ་ཞིང་བྱམས་པ་ཆེན་པོའི་ཏིང་འཛིན་རྒྱུད་ལ་ལྷང་གིས་སྐྱེས་པར་བསམ། མཉམ་ཉིད་ཡེ་ཤེས་ཀྱི་རང་གདངས་རིན་ཆེན་རིགས་ཀྱི་མཁའ་འགྲོ་མ་སེར་མོ་དགའ་སྤྲོ་དགྱེས་པའི་ཉམས་དང་ལྡན་པས་རིག་རྩལ་སྙིང་རྗེ་ཆེན་པོའི་ཕུར་པ་སེར་པོ་གྲུ་བཞིའི་རྣམ་པ་ཅན་ང་རྒྱལ་གྱི་རང་བཞིན་ལག་གཡོན་པར་བཏབ་པས་ང་རྒྱལ་རྒྱགས་པའི་རྟོག་པ་སྐད་ཅིག་ཀྱང་མི་གཡོ་ཞིང་སྙིང་རྗེ་ཆེན་པོའི་ཏིང་འཛིན་རྒྱུད་ལ་སྐྱེས་པར་བསམ། རང་རིག་སོར་རྟོག་ཡེ་ཤེས་ཀྱི་རང་གདངས་པདྨ་རིགས་ཀྱི་མཁའ་འགྲོ་མ་དམར་མོ་འཛུམ་ཆགས་བཞད་པའི་ཉམས་དང་ལྡན་པས་དགའ་བ་ཆེན་པོའི་རང་བཞིན་དབང་གི་ཕུར་པ་ཟླ་གམ་གི་རྣམ་པ་ཅན་འདོད་ཆགས་ཀྱི་རང་བཞིན་རྐང་པ་གཡོན་པར་བཏབ་པས་འདོད་ཆགས་ཞེན་པའི་རྟོག་པ་སྐད་ཅིག་ཀྱང་མི་གཡོ་ཞིང་དགའ་བ་ཆེན་པོའི་ཏིང་འཛིན་རྒྱུད་ལ་སྐྱེས་པར་བསམ། རང་རིག་བྱ་གྲུབ་ཡེ་ཤེས་ཀྱི་རང་གདངས་ལས་ཀྱི་མཁའ་འགྲོ་མ་ལྗང་མོ་ཁྲོ་གཉུམ་འཁྲུགས་པའི་ཉམས་དང་ལྡན་པས་རིག་རྩལ་བཏང་སྙོམས་ཆེན་པོའི་རང་བཞིན་དྲག་པོའི་ཕུར་པ་ནག་པོ་གྲུ་གསུམ་གྱི་རྣམ་པར་ཕྲག་དོག་གི་རང་བཞིན་རྐང་པ་གཡས་པར་བཏབ་པས་ཕྲག་དོག་འགྲན་སེམས་ཀྱི་རྟོག་པ་སྐད་ཅིག་ཀྱང་མི་གཡོ་ཞིང་བཏང་སྙོམས་ཆེན་པོའི་ཏིང་འཛིན་རྒྱུད་ལ་སྐྱེས་པར་བསམ། རང་རིག་ཆོས་དབྱིངས་ཡེ་ཤེས་ཀྱི་རང་གདངས་སངས་རྒྱས་རིགས་ཀྱི་མཁའ་འགྲོ་མ་མཐིང་ག་དགའ་ཁྲོ་ཆགས་པའི་ཉམས་འགྱུར་རྫོགས་པའི་རིག་རྩལ་སྨོན་འཇུག་བྱང་ཆུབ་སེམས་ཀྱི་རང་བཞིན་ཕུར་བུ་ཆངས་ཟུང་ཟླུམ་པོ་རྒྱ་མདུད་གྲུ་བཞི་དཔལ་ཁ་ཟླ་གམ་དཔལ་རྩེ་གྲུ་གསུམ་སྟེ་ལས་བཞི་ལྷུན་གྲུབ་ཀྱི་རྣམ་པ་ཅན་གཏི་མུག་མ་རིག་པའི་རང་བཞིན་མགོ་བོར་བཏབ་པས་གཟུང་འཛིན་གྱི་དབང་གིས་ལུས་ངག་ཡིད་གསུམ་སྐད་ཅིག་ཀྱང་མི་གཡོ་ཞིང་བྱང་ཆུབ་སེམས་ཀྱི་ངང་དུ་ལྷན་གྱིས་གནས་པར་

བསམས་ནས་ཕུར་གདབ་བྱའོ། །དེ་ལྟར་འཕྲུལ་གཟུགས་ལྷ་འདྲེར་སྣང་བ་གནས་རྟེན་དང་བཅས་པ་ཐམས་ཅད་ཡེ་ཤེས་ལྔའི་ཀློང་དུ་སྦྱངས་ནས། ཡུམ་ལྔའི་མཁའ་ཀློང་གི་རང་བཞིན་དུ་རྣམ་པར་དག་པའི་དབྱིངས་སུ་ཅིག་བུ་མཁའ་འགྲོའི་ཕོ་བྲང་བཅས་འཁོར་བ་མ་སྟོང་གི་བར་དུ་གནས་པར་བྱའོ་སྙམ་དུ་ཡང་ཡང་བསམ་ཞིང་མཐར་བདག་གནས་ལྷ་འདྲེ་དང་བཅས་པ་གང་དུའང་མི་དམིགས་ཤིང་། རིག་སྟོང་སྤྲོས་པ་དང་བྲལ་བའི་ངང་དུ་ཡུམ་དོན་ཤེས་རབ་ཕར་ཕྱིན་གྱི་ཉམས་ལེན་ལས་སྐད་ཅིག་ཀྱང་མི་གཡེང་བས་བསྐྱང་བར་བྱའོ། །འདི་གཉིས་ཀ་ལ་བདག་གནས་ལྷ་འདྲེ་ཟིལ་གྱིས་གནོན་པ་གསུམ་ཀ་ཚང་ཡང་གཙོ་ཆེ་བའི་དབང་དུ་བྱས་ནས་བྲོ་བརྡུང་གིས་བདག་དང་གནས་ཟིལ་གྱིས་གནོན་པ་དང་ཕུར་གདབ་ཀྱིས་ལྷ་འདྲེ་ཟིལ་གྱིས་གནོན་པ་གཙོ་བོར་སྟོན་པས་ཟིལ་གནོན་སྐོར་གསུམ་ལོགས་ནས་བཙལ་མི་དགོས། དེ་ལྟར་ཟིལ་གནོན་གྱི་དམིགས་པ་ལ་བརྟེན་ནས་ལྡོང་དང་ཆོ་འཕྲུལ་རྣམས་ཁྲིད་གཞུང་ནས་བཤད་པ་ལྟར་བྱུང་བ་དང་། ཉམས་ལེན་ཕུང་པོ་ཟན་བསྐྱུར་དངོས་ལ་འཇུག་པ་སྟེ། དེ་ལ་ཡང་སྔོན་འགྲོ་དངོས་གཞི་རྗེས་གསུམ་ལས། དང་པོ་སྔོན་འགྲོ་ལ་བཞི་ལས་སྐྱབས་སུ་འགྲོ་བ་ནི། རང་ཉིད་ཐ་མལ་དུ་གནས་པའི་མདུན་གྱི་ནམ་མཁར་རྩ་བའི་བླ་མ་དེ་ཉིད་ཆོས་སྐུ་རྡོ་རྗེ་འཆང་ཆེན་པོའི་རྣམ་པར་བཞུགས་པའི་མཐའ་བསྐོར་དུ་རྒྱལ་བ་དགོངས་པའི་བརྒྱུད་པ། རིག་འཛིན་བརྡའི་བརྒྱུད་པ། གང་ཟག་སྙན་ཁུངས་བརྒྱུད་པའི་བླ་མ་རྣམས་དང་ཡི་དམ་དཀྱིལ་འཁོར་གྱི་ལྷ་ཚོགས་མཁའ་འགྲོ་ཆོས་སྐྱོང་སྲུང་མའི་ཚོགས་དང་བཅས་པ་ཐམས་ཅད་ནམ་མཁའི་སྤྲིན་ཕུང་འཁྲིགས་པ་ལྟར་བཞུགས་པའི་དྲུང་དུ་རང་གི་འཁོར་དུ་གནས་གདོན་ལུས་གདོན་ལས་གདོན་གསུམ་གྱིས་ཐོག་དྲངས་རིགས་དྲུག་གི་སེམས་ཅན་ཐམས་ཅད་ཁྲིམ་འཚོགས་པ་ལྟར་ཚོགས་ནས་ལུས་ངག་ཡིད་གསུམ་ཆུན་གཅིག་དྲིལ་གྱི་སྐྱབས་འགྲོ་བྱེད་པར་བསམ་ཞིང་སྐྱབས་འགྲོ་བྱ། གཉིས་པ་སེམས་བསྐྱེད་ནི། སྤྱིར་སྨོན་འཇུག་སོགས་ཀྱི་གོ་བ་ཁྲིད་གཞུང་ལྟར་ཤེས་པར་བྱ་ཞིང་གསལ་འདེབས་དང་། ཁྱད་པར་རང་གཞན་སེམས་ཅན་ཐམས་ཅད་ཐོག་མ་མེད་པའི་དུས་ནས་ཕྱི་སྣང་བའི་ཡུལ་ལ་དངོས་པོ་བདེན་གྲུབ་ཏུ་ཞེན་ཏེ། དགག་སྒྲུབ་

ཆགས་སྣང་གི་དབང་དུ་གྱུར་པས། དེ་ཉིད་རིག་པ་བརྟུལ་ཞུགས་ཀྱི་སྤྱོད་པས་ཚར་
བཅད་ནས་ཡང་དག་པའི་གནས་ལུགས་རྟོགས་པར་བྱའོ་སྙམ་དུ་སེམས་བསྐྱེད།
གསུམ་པ་མཐྲུལ་ནི། གཞུང་གཞན་ནས་ཐེམ་རིག་ཁྲོལ་ཏེ་པགས་པ་བཤུས་ནས་
དབང་ཆེན་གསེར་གྱིས་གཞིར་བསྒོམ་པ་སོགས་རིམ་བཞིན་གསལ་འདེབས་པར་
གསུངས་ཀྱང་། འདིར་ཐེམ་རིག་ཁྲོལ་བ་མ་གསུངས་པ་ལུས་གཅེས་པར་འཛིན་
མཁན་གྱི་སེམས་དེ་ཉིད་འབུལ་བ་པོར་བྱས་ནས་གཅེས་པར་བཟུང་རྒྱུའི་ལུས་ཡན་ལག་
ཉིང་ལག་ལ་སོགས་པ་གླིང་བཞི་རི་རབ་ཉི་ཟླ་སོགས་བློས་བཏགས་ཏེ་གཅེས་འཛིན་དང་
བྲལ་བས་ཚོགས་ཞིང་གི་ལྷ་ཚོགས་རྣམས་ལ་འབུལ་ཏེ་རྣམ་པ་གསལ་ཀྱང་ལེགས་ལ་མ་
གསལ་ཀྱང་འདྲ། བཞི་པ་བླ་མའི་རྣལ་འབྱོར་ནི། རང་གཞན་སེམས་ཅན་ཐམས་
ཅད་ཀྱི་མདུན་གྱི་ནམ་མཁའ་རྩ་བརྒྱུད་བླ་མ་འདུས་པའི་རང་བཞིན་ཨོ་རྒྱན་རྡོ་རྗེ་འཆང་
ཧེ་རུ་ཀའི་ཆས་ཅན་དུ་གསལ་བ་ལ་བདག་གཞན་སེམས་ཅན་ཐམས་ཅད་མགྲིན་གཅིག་
ཏུ་སྙིང་ཁོང་རུས་པའི་གཏིང་ནས་གསོལ་བ་གདབ། མཐར་རྩ་བའི་བླ་མའི་གསང་
གསུམ་དང་རང་གི་སྒོ་གསུམ་དུ་མ་རོ་གཅིག་ཏུ་གྱུར་པར་བསམས་ལ་གནས་ལུགས་ཀྱི་
ངང་ལ་མཉམ་པར་གཞག་གོ །ཏེ་ཡན་ཆད་སྔོན་འགྲོའི་རྣམ་པ་སོང་ནས། གཉིས་
པ་དངོས་གཞི་ཐེམ་རིག་ཁྲོལ་ནས་ཁྲོས་མ་བསྐྱེད་པ། མགྲོན་རྣམས་སྤྱན་འདྲེན་པ།
འགྱེད་ཆེན་གསུམ་མམ་བཞི་བྱ་བའོ། །དང་པོ་རང་གི་ལུས་འདི་ཉིད་ཆེ་ལ་ཚོ་ཞིང་
སྣུམ་ལ་གཞོན་ཞིང་ལང་ཚོ་མཛེས་པའི་སྙིང་གའི་དབུས་སུ་རང་སེམས་ཀྱི་ངོ་བོ་མ་ཅིག་
ཁྲོས་མ་ནག་མོ་གར་སྟབས་ལེང་ངེ་བར་གསལ་བ་དེ་ཉིད་ཕཊ༔ ཅེས་བརྗོད་པས་སྤྱི་
བོ་ཚངས་པའི་བུ་ག་ནས་ནམ་མཁར་སྤར། དེའི་ཕྱག་གི་གྲི་གུག་གིས་རང་གི་སྨིན་
མཚམས་ནས་བྲེགས་ཏེ་ཕྱག་གཡོན་པས་བླངས་ནས་ཐོད་པའི་སྒྱེད་པུ་རི་རབ་དང་མཉམ་
པ་གསུམ་གྱི་སྟེང་དུ་བཀལ་བ་སྟོང་གསུམ་རྒྱ་ཁྱོན་དང་མཉམ་པར་གྱུར་པའི་ནང་དུ་རང་
ལུས་རིམ་པ་བཞིན་གྲི་གུག་གིས་གཏུབས་ནས་བཅུག་པའི་འོག་ནས་རླུང་གཡོས་མེ་སྦར་
ཤ་ཁྲག་རུས་གསུམ་བདུད་རྩིའི་རང་བཞིན་དུ་ཞུ་བར་ཨོཾ་ཨཱཿཧཱུྃ་གི་བྱིན་གྱིས་བརླབ་པ་
གཞུང་ལྟར་བྱ། གཉིས་པ་མགྲོན་འབོད་པ་ནི། རང་ཉིད་ཁྲོས་མའི་ཐུགས་ཀའི་

འོད་ཟེར་གྱིས་བཀུག་ནས་ཡར་མཆོད་ཡུལ་དུ་གྱུར་པའི་བླ་མ་ཡི་དམ་མཁའ་འགྲོ་
སངས་རྒྱས་བྱང་སེམས་ལ་སོགས་པ་ནས་བཟུང་སྐྱེ་མར་སྦྱིན་ཡུལ་དུ་གྱུར་པའི་ལྷ་འདྲེ་
གདོན་བགེགས་ཡན་ཆད་གནམ་ས་བར་སྣང་ཐམས་ཅད་གང་བར་འདུས་པར་བསམ་
ཞིང་། མཆོད་ཡུལ་དམ་ཅན་སོགས་བརྗོད། གསུམ་པ་འགྱེད་ཆེན་གྱི་དམིགས་པ་
སྤྱིར་མགྲོན་རིགས་ཐམས་ཅད་ལ་དཀར་འགྱེད་དང་། ཁྲ་འགྱེད་གཉིས་བྱེད་པ་དང་།
ཁྱད་པར་ཤ་ཁྲག་ཟ་བའི་རིགས་ལ་དམར་འགྱེད། གདོན་བགེགས་ལ་ནག་འགྱེད་
བྱེད་པ་སོགས་དམིགས་པའི་རྣམ་གྲངས་རྣམས་ཤེས་པར་བྱ་ཞིང་། རང་གཞུང་འདོན་
ཆ་དང་སྦྲགས་ནས་ཡར་མགྲོན་རྣམས་ལ་དཀར་འགྱེད་བདུད་རྩིའི་རང་བཞིན་དུ་སྟོང་བ་
དང་། མར་མགྲོན་ལྷ་འདྲེ་གདོན་བགེགས་འབྱུང་པོ་ཡི་དྭགས་སྲིན་པོ་སོགས་ལ་
དམར་འགྱེད་ཤ་ཁྲག་རུས་གསུམ་སོགས་བསྔོ་བ་དང་། རིགས་དྲུག་གཞན་དང་བུ་
ལོན་ལན་ཆགས་ཀྱི་བདག་པོ་རྣམས་ལ་ཁྲ་འགྱེད་གང་ལ་གང་འདོད་དུ་འདོད་རྒུའི་ཆར་
འབེབས་པ་སོགས་ཡིན་ཏེ་དམིགས་པའི་རྣམ་གྲངས་ནི་གཅོད་གཞུང་རྣམས་དང་ཁྲིད་
ཡིག་ལས་ཤེས་པར་བྱའོ། །གསུམ་པ་རྗེས་བསྔོ་བ་དང་སྨོན་ལམ་བྱ་བ་ནི།
གཏོང་ལེན་གྱི་བདག་གཞན་བརྗེ་བ་ཆོས་ཀྱི་སྦྱིན་པས་སྦྱིན་གཏོང་དོན་ཆེན་པོར་བྱེད་པ་
སོགས་རྒྱལ་སྲས་སྤྱིའི་གཞུང་ལམ་ལྟར་ཉམས་སུ་བླང་བར་བྱའོ། །དེ་ལྟར་ཐུན་དྲུག་
གམ་བཞི་ལ་སོགས་པར་ལུས་སྦྱིན་བྱ་ཞིང་གཙོ་བོར་ལུས་ལ་གཅེས་འཛིན་དང་།
སེམས་ལ་བདག་འཛིན་གྱི་བློ་དྲུང་ནས་ཕྱུང་སྟེ་སུས་འདོད་པ་ཁྱེར། ཅི་ཡོང་བ་ཤོག
སླམ་དུ་སླེམ་བྱེད་བདག་གི་འཕྲི་བ་ཆོད་པའི་ལྟ་བའི་ངང་སྐྱོང་ཞིང་། སྟོང་ཉིད་སྙིང་རྗེ་
དང་འབྲེལ་པའི་སྒོ་ནས་ཚད་མེད་བཞིའི་ཏིང་ངེ་འཛིན་ལ་གཙོ་བོར་འབད་པར་བྱའོ། །
གཅོད་ནི་ཡུམ་དོན་ཤེས་རབ་ཕར་ཕྱིན་གྱི་དགོངས་པ་སྟོང་ཉིད་སྙིང་རྗེའི་སྙིང་པོ་ཅན་ལ་
ཉམས་ལེན་གྱི་མཐིལ་དུ་བྱེད་པ་ཡིན་པས་གཙོ་བོར་སྙིང་རྗེ་ཆེན་པོའི་སྒོ་ནས་ཞི་དུལ་བག་
ཡོད་དང་ལྡན་པས་ཉམས་སུ་བླང་ཞིང་། འབྲེལ་ཚད་དགེ་ལ་འགྱུར་ཏེ་ལྷ་འདྲེའི་འགྲོ་
དོན་ནུས་པ་ཞིག་དགོས་ཀྱི། ཞེ་སྡང་གི་སྡང་མིག་གཡོ་བས་ལྷ་འདྲེ་བསྒྲད་བརྡུང་བྱེད་
པ་ནི་གཅོད་ལོག་བདུད་དུ་སོང་ནས་ངན་སོང་དུ་འགྲོ་བ་ནི་མ་ཅིག་གི་ལུང་བསྟན་སོགས་

ལས་ཤེས་པར་བྱ་ཞིང་།   སྔོན་འགྲོའི་སྦྱངས་པ་རྣམས་མཐར་ཕྱིན་པ་དང་།   དངོས་གཞིའི་ཉམས་ལེན་གཉིས་ལ་སྦྱོང་བ་ཅུང་ཟད་ཀྱང་མ་སྐྱེས་ཤིང་སྙིང་རྗེ་ཆེན་པོའི་རྩིས་མ་ཟིན་པར་གཉན་ས་སོགས་འགྲིམ་སྤྱ་ན་ལྷ་འདྲེས་རྒྱུད་བརླམས་ནས་ལྟར་སྣང་གི་མངོན་ཤེས་དག་ནུས་སོགས་འབྱུང་ཡང་ཤེས་རྒྱུད་ཆོས་དང་ཅི་འགལ་དུ་འགྲོ་ཞིང་།   འདི་སྣང་གི་གྲུབ་ཐོབ་ཆེན་པོ་ནི་དམྱལ་བའི་གྲོང་སྒྲོར་འོ་བརྒྱལ་ཆེ་བ་ཡང་ཤེས་དགོས་སོ།   །དེས་ན་དུས་དང་རྣམ་པ་ཐམས་ཅད་དུ་བླ་མ་དཀོན་མཆོག་ལ་ཁྱེད་ཤེས་ཀྱི་དད་པ།   འགྲོ་དྲུག་གི་སེམས་ཅན་ལ་བརྩེས་མིན་གྱི་སྙིང་རྗེ།   རི་དྭགས་ཀྱི་འཛིན་པ་ལ་རོ་སྙོམས་ཀྱི་གདོང་བརྡེག་བྱེད་པ་དང་མ་བྲལ་བའི་ངང་ནས་ཉམས་ལེན་ཕུང་པོ་གཟན་བསྐྱུར་ལ་འབད་ཅིང་།   རྒྱལ་བའི་བཀའ་དང་འགྲེལ་པའི་ཆོས་སྦྱིན་དང་།   འགྲེལ་ཚད་དགེ་ལ་འགོད་པའི་སྨོན་ལམ་གཉིས་ལ་ནན་ཏན་བྱེད་ཅིང་བདག་ལས་ལྷ་འདྲེ་གཅེས་པར་བཟུང་ནས་རང་གཞན་གཉིས་ཀའི་རྒྱུད་ཀྱི་དུག་ལྔ་ལ་གཅོད་པར་བྱེད་པ་ནི་རྒྱལ་བ་སྲས་བཅས་དགྱེས་པའི་གཅོད་ཡུལ་གྱི་ལམ་བཟང་མ་ནོར་བ་ཡིན་ནོ།   །མཚུངས་མེད་དམ་པ་དུ་མའི་བཀའ་དྲིན་ལས།   །དབང་ཐོབ་བདུད་རྩི་བཏུང་བས་སྙིང་སེམ་ཡང་།   །ཉམས་སྦྱོང་ཟུངས་སུ་མ་ལོན་སྐལ་དམན་བདག   །ཟབ་དོན་མན་ངག་འཆད་ལ་ཇི་ལྟར་དབང་།   །དེ་ལྟ་ན་ཡང་སྙིགས་མའི་དུས་མཐའ་འདིར།   །རྒྱལ་བ་དགྱེས་པའི་ལམ་ལ་རྒྱབ་ཕྱོགས་པའི།   །དྲག་ཤུལ་བདུད་ཀྱིས་བརླམས་པའི་གཅོད་ཀན་ལས།   །ཉམ་ཆུང་བདག་འདྲ་སྐལ་བ་བཟང་ངམ་སྙམ།   །དེ་འདྲ་དེ་ཡང་བླ་མ་རྗེ་ཡི་དྲིན།   །དྲིན་ལན་འཁོར་མཐའ་མེད་དོ་ཆོས་ཀྱི་རྗེ།   །རྟག་ཏུ་མི་བརྗེད་དད་པའི་གདུང་ཤུགས་ཀྱིས།   །ཡང་ཡང་གསོལ་བ་འདེབས་སོ་བྱིན་གྱིས་རློབས།   །དེ་ལྟར་གཅོད་ཡུལ་མཁའ་འགྲོའི་གད་རྒྱངས་འདི་ཉིད་རང་གཞུང་ཞལ་གསལ་བ་དང་།   ཁྱད་པར་དཔལ་གྲུབ་པའི་དབང་ཕྱུག་ལག་ན་རྡོ་རྗེ་དང་།   སྲས་ཀྱི་ཐུ་བོ་ཨཱནནྡ་དེ་བ་སྟེ་གྲུབ་རྗེ་བ་སྲས་གཉིས་ཀྱི་གཞུང་ཁྲིད་རྣམ་བཤད་སོགས་དང་།   ཁྱད་པར་དབང་སྡུད་ཟིལ་གནོན་སྒོར་རྒྱས་བསྡུས་ཀྱི་ཡི་གེ་གྲངས་མང་བ་བཅས་ན།   ཡན་ལག་བརྒྱད་ལྡན་གྱི་མཚོ་འགྲམ་དུ།   བ་རྩྭའི་ཁྲིན་བརྙོ་མ་དགོས་ཀྱང་སྐུལ་བ་པོའི་བཀའ་ཕེབས་

ཕྱོག་ཏུ་མ་ནུས་ནས་ཉམས་སུ་མ་ཡོན་པའི་ཆོས་བཤད་འོན་པའི་རོལ་མོ་ལྷ་བུར་བྲིས་
པའོ། །དགེའོ། །དགེའོ། །དགེའོ།།

Index

accumulation field 6, 7, 42, 45, 48
activity dakinis 79
actual giving of the body . . . 5, 40
actuality 6, 43, 44, 86, 87, 95
actuality of reality . . 6, 43, 44, 86
Adzom Drukpa . . . . xx, 119
afflicted energy 34, 35
affliction 35, 36, 38, 95
aggregate 6, 45, 73
alaya . . . . ix, 95, 96
all-accomplishing wisdom . . 4, 37
all-inclusive space vi
amrita 8, 51, 54
Andreas Kretschmar ix
appearance 2, 20, 23, 29, 31, 41, 46, 60-62, 67, 68, 75, 76, 78, 79, 81, 92, 96-98, 105, 111
arena of cutting 16
arouse the mind 6, 43, 85
arousing enlightenment mind 41, 43
aspiration . . . x, 12, 66, 67, 90, 92
aspiring mind 85
assurance . . . 2, 10, 12, 28-32, 59, 60, 64, 74, 96
assurance of the view . . 2, 12, 30, 64, 74
assurance of yogic activity 2, 29, 30, 32
attitude of brave assurance . . . 28
attitude of bravery 2, 27, 28
aurally heard lineage of ordinary persons 41
awareness 5, 37, 38, 86, 88, 108, 112
becoming . . 2, 31, 55, 75, 77, 82, 91, 96
bells . . . 1, 4, 9, 22, 25, 37, 55, 79
black distribution 8, 11, 52, 61, 89
Black Wrathful Woman 8, 52, 88
bodhichitta 27, 85
body dakinis 78
body dons 81, 85
body of elements 8, 50
body of latencies 7, 49
Brahma aperture 88
brave assurance 28
buddha dakini 5, 39
buddhahood . . . . vi, 99, 111, 112
Buddhist tantras vii
carpet of flesh and bones . . 11, 63
cast aside attachment to the body xiv
casting aside the aggregate body 73
casting aside the body as food . . . . xix, xx, 1, 21, 84
charnel grounds xvi

chen po 15, 102
chevrons of hair 1, 22
Chod . . i, iii, v, xiii-xxii, xxiv, xxv, xxviii, 1, 15-19, 21-29, 33, 35, 38, 40, 44, 46-48, 53, 54, 57, 59, 61, 62, 64-66, 68, 70-73, 78, 83, 84, 86-94
  certainty of 64
  enhancement practice 62
  essential theme . . . . xiv, xv
  finishing 64
  how the view is presented . xv
  Longchen Nyingthig . xiv, xvi
  Pacifier . . . . xiv, xv
  provoking upheavals 64
  temporary experiences of . 65
  visualization procedures . . xxii
  yogic conduct . . . . xv, xvi
Chod damarus xvii
Chod practice . i, iii, xiii-xvii, xx, xxii, xxiv, 1, 15-17, 19, 23, 24, 26-29, 35, 40, 46, 53, 59, 62, 64-66, 71, 72, 93
Chod practice of Longchen Nyingthig xvi
Chod Practice Sound of Dakini Laughter . . iii, xiv, xxii, 15, 17, 72, 93
Chogyam Trungpa . . . . . vii, xxv, 108, 109, 113
city of hell 91
cleaning washerwoman 79
clinging 75, 79, 80, 82, 97
code words 25, 55
communication from the dharmakaya 19
compassion . . . 5, 10, 13, 21, 39, 58, 59, 67, 68, 74-76, 78, 80-82, 90-92, 101, 106
compassionate activity 75
complete purity . . . 71, 72, 83, 97
complexity . . . . xx, 105
concept labels 12, 66, 97
concept of cutter xix
concepts . . . 12, 21, 40, 66, 92, 97
conclusion 12, 66, 72, 84, 90, 108
condescending stance . . 2, 27, 73
conduct of yogic activity . . . xviii, xx, 1, 6, 13, 20, 43, 44, 67
confidence . . . . xi, 28, 31, 96
confusion . . vi, 13, 67, 75, 76, 97
contagious disease 11, 63
cosmos 49
cosmos described by the Buddha 49
Creation of the Wrathful Woman 88
cutter and cut . . . . xviii, 1, 20
Cutter of Mara 7, 48
Cutter's Object 12, 65, 66
Dalai Lama xxi
damaru 1, 22, 25
dance 3-5, 33-37, 75, 77-82
dance floor . . . 3-5, 35-37, 80, 81
dance floor of the dakas and dakinis 3-5, 35-37
Death Demon 5, 36, 37
death demons 81
debts . . . 10, 13, 54, 58, 59, 66, 89
debts of retribution 10, 13, 58, 66
deceiving adulteress 79
dedication . . 9, 12, 56, 58, 66, 67
degree of expanse 11, 62
deities of the accumulation field 6, 45
demons and dons of retribution 8, 53
Derge Printing House xxii
desire realm 75
dharma protectors 9, 42, 56

dharmadhatu wisdom 5, 37
dharmakaya . . xi, 7, 9, 13, 18, 19, 36, 43, 45, 46, 48, 57, 66, 67, 75, 79, 84, 98, 115
dharmakaya's space 7, 45
dharmapalas 6, 41, 85
diacritical marks . . . . ii, xxvi
Dilgo Khyentse . . . . . xiii, xx, xxvi
Direct Crossing . . . . xvi, 115
discriminating wisdom 4, 37, 107
discursive thought . . 3, 7, 33, 48, 79, 98
distributions of the body 51
Dodrupchen . . . . xx, 115
dons . . . xv, 2, 8, 9, 12, 31, 52-54, 57, 64, 76, 80-82, 85, 89
dualistic ignorance 41, 55
dualistic ignorance of self-grasping 41
dualistic mind . . . vii, xiii, 21, 40, 45, 57, 85, 97, 99, 101, 106, 107, 111, 112
dualistic thinking 3, 33, 34
Dza Patrul . . iii, viii, xiv, xxii, 17, 71, 88, 93, 115
Dzogchen . . xix, xxii, xxx, 15, 56, 115, 125
eight classes of elementals . . 8, 9, 53, 57
eight worldly concerns 2, 27
elaborate practices xviii
elaboration 22, 99
electronic editions 115, 116
electronic texts 116
elementals 8, 9, 53, 57
empowerment . . . xii, xv, 92, 115
  infinite luminous purity . . . xii
emptiness . . . xvii, 10, 11, 20, 40, 41, 45, 51, 59, 60, 63, 65-67, 76, 78, 81, 90, 92, 94, 99-101, 104-106, 111
enlightened activity . . 13, 67, 76, 112
enlightenment . 5, 22, 23, 27, 28, 39, 40, 43, 44, 46, 68, 75, 77, 81, 83, 85, 96, 99-101, 103, 105, 110-112
enlightenment mind . . 5, 27, 39, 41, 43, 44, 68, 81, 83, 85, 96, 99-101, 110
  two types 44
  ultimate 44
enmeshing fetters 77
entity 6, 43, 60, 99, 100
equipoise . . . 5, 7, 10, 12, 40, 48, 59, 64, 67, 84, 87
equipoise of the non-dual state 7, 48
essence . 7, 19, 21, 23, 46, 47, 88, 99, 100, 104, 106, 111
expanse . . . . x-xii, xv, xvii, 1, 5, 7, 10-12, 20, 41, 42, 45, 46, 48, 60, 62, 64, 72, 74, 75, 77, 79, 82, 83, 100
expanse and luminosity 42
expanse and rigpa 12, 64
expanse dharmakaya 7, 48
expanse of emptiness 45, 60
expanse without outflows . . 7, 45
expanse's luminosity 41
fearful hesitation 10, 59
fearless behaviour of an ordinary person 33
fearless yogic activity 3, 33
feast 8, 9, 50, 53, 54
  follows the distributions . . 53
  guests must be summoned . 53
  higher beings 53
  lower beings 53
feast substance 50

feminine principle 20
fictional . 12, 44, 66, 68, 96, 100, 101, 110
fictional truth 100, 110
field of refuge 48
final realization . . . . vi, 76
final space of realization vi
finishing 12, 64, 65
first-order thousandfold 110
five aggregates 77
five amritas 51
five buddha families 34
five buddhas 41
five dry skulls 77
five families 41, 77
five kayas 51, 77
five paramitas 77
five poisons 77, 92
five sense objects ix
five symbolic ornaments 77
five wisdoms 36, 51, 83
flaying knife 7, 49, 88
flesh and bones . . . 11, 12, 63, 64
flesh, blood, and bones . 9, 58, 89
flesh-eating dons 9, 57
Flower Cave of Great Secrecy . . . . ix, xi
focus . . . . xix, 5, 37, 61, 101
foremost instructions . . . iii, xiv, xix, xx, xxii, 1, 17, 21, 22, 71, 92, 93, 101
form realm 75
formless peak of existence 74
four and six tantra sections . . . 78
four continents . . . 6, 44, 86, 110
four immeasurables . 2, 27, 39, 81
four maras 16, 72
four types of maras 60
four ways of going 2, 30
fruition realization 45
fully-informed refuge 6, 42
garuda . . . . xviii, 115
generosity . 8, 12, 13, 53, 57, 66, 68, 90, 92
generosity of giving dharma . . 90
generosity of the fictional body 12, 66
god abodes 6, 44
Godaniya 4, 37, 80
gods and demons . . . xx, xxv, 1-3, 5, 6, 8-11, 13, 22-24, 26-28, 30-34, 38-40, 42, 52, 53, 56, 60, 62-64, 67-69, 73, 74, 77, 81-84, 91, 92
gods and demons of self-grasping 3, 5, 33, 39
grasped-grasping 83, 101
grasping at a self . . . . xiv, xix, 11, 24, 34, 45, 61
great . . . . . v-xv, xvii-xx, xxii, xxiii, xxv, 1, 5, 9, 12, 13, 15, 20-22, 25, 29, 30, 32-36, 39-41, 47, 48, 54-57, 64, 65, 67-69, 71, 72, 74-78, 80-86, 88, 89, 91, 93, 95, 96, 98-109, 111, 113-115, 125
great bliss . ix, 1, 5, 20, 41, 75, 78
great compassion . . 5, 13, 39, 68, 74, 76, 78, 80, 82, 91, 101
Great Completion . v-viii, x, xiii-xv, xvii-xx, xxii, xxv, 1, 15, 20, 21, 29, 30, 33, 47, 48, 55, 57, 64, 65, 67-69, 72, 93, 95, 96, 98, 102-108, 111, 114, 115
  direct experience of alpha purity xv
  Longchen Nyingthig viii
  mother xviii
  Nyingthig . . . vii, viii, xvii, 47, 64, 93

quintessential viii
great equanimity ... 5, 39, 81-83
great expanse of realization ... xi
great grounds 56, 125
great grounds' trumpet . 9, 55, 56
Great Humkara xi
great joy 5, 39, 80-82
great loving kindness 5, 39, 80, 82
Great Perfection 102
great supreme 1, 9, 22, 54
Great Vajradhara 84
Great Vehicle 71, 72, 85, 99, 100, 102, 103
guards 6, 41, 42, 85
guest 59
guru yoga .... viii, 6, 45, 87
gurus . 3, 6, 9, 16, 34, 41, 56, 63, 78, 84, 87, 89, 114
Gyalpo 3, 35, 80
harmful appearance 60
haughtiness 77, 80
haughty ones 1, 22, 23
head of anger 3, 35
head of arrogance 4, 37
head of desire 4, 37
head of ignorance 5, 37
head of jealousy 4, 37
heaps of a mandala 6, 45
herding animals into a pen ... 31
herding goats and sheep ... 2, 31
heruka 7, 9, 45, 46, 57, 87
heruka in style 9, 57
higher being guests 89
higher beings 53, 54, 56
holier than though attitudes 10, 60
hope and fear ... 6, 7, 12, 43, 44, 48, 66, 81, 92
human .. 3, 9, 11, 18, 25, 26, 33, 55-58, 63, 76, 89, 94, 125
human hide 9, 57, 58, 76
human skin 11, 63
human thighbone trumpet ... 3, 33, 56, 76, 125
Humkara xi
humming of a bee 14
ignorance .. 5, 36, 37, 41, 49, 55, 76, 83, 97, 100, 105, 106
Illuminator Tibetan-English Dictionary 77, 87, 94, 114, 117
impure portion 7, 49
inexhaustible wheel of ornamentation 74, 75
infallible interdependency 12, 66
interdependent arising ix
items appropriate to the yogic activity 2, 22
Jambudvipa 4, 36, 80
jealous thoughts 81
Jigmey Gyalway Nyugu viii
Jigmey Lingpa .. i, iii, viii, ix, xiii, xvii, xviii, xx, xxi, xxiii, xxvi, xxx, 1, 18, 19, 23, 47, 84, 88, 115
juncture vi
kapala 8, 54
karma dakini 5, 39, 82
karmic debts 54, 58, 59, 89
karmic latencies 49
karmic retribution 54
khatvanga ..... xvii, 1, 22, 24, 25
kila 38
Lama Wangdu .... xxi, 18
lasso of snakes and intestines 12, 63
latencies .... xi, 7, 12, 49, 65, 74, 75, 77, 79
laughter ... iii, xiv, xxii, 1, 15, 17-19, 71, 72, 78, 93
liberating activity 29
life demons 81
lineage gurus .. 6, 16, 41, 63, 78,

84, 87
little bells . 1, 4, 9, 22, 25, 37, 55, 79
lived space of emptiness 65
liveliness 80-83, 103, 106
Longchen Nyingthig .... i, iii, v, viii, xiii-xviii, xx, xxii, 1, 15, 16, 18, 78, 86, 89, 119
Longchen Rabjam ... viii, xx, 15
Longchenpa .... viii, xi-xiii
All Knowing Lord xii
Lord of Speech ix
praise to xiii
Seven Treasuries ..... x, xiii
Three Chariots xiii
wisdom body viii
Longchenpa's wisdom body . viii
Lord of Death 4, 35-37
Lord of Speech ix
love and compassion 13, 67
lower being guests 59, 89
lower beings 53, 54, 56-59
Lower Cave of Nyang ..... ix, xi
luminosity .... ix, xix, 5, 7, 9, 41, 42, 46, 47, 57, 98, 104, 105, 111
luminosity nature xix
luminosity-great bliss 5, 41
lustre .. 7, 13, 45, 46, 67, 68, 104
lustre of the view 68
Machig Labdron xiv
maha v, 72, 95, 102, 104-109, 111
mahasandhi .... v, 102
main part .. 40, 72, 84, 87, 88, 91
main part of the practice 40
malevolent demons 11, 63
malevolent gods and demons . 5, 38, 63, 82
mandala ... xii, 6, 33, 40, 44, 45, 85, 86
mandala of the deity 33, 40
mandala offering 44, 86
Manjushrimitra xi
mara ... 7, 10, 16, 17, 19, 23, 35, 48, 60, 66, 72, 76, 91, 93, 105
merit and wisdom 45, 77
message of blissful wisdom ... 18
meteoric iron ... 2, 5, 30, 38, 39, 73, 105
mind dakinis 78
mind lineage of the conquerors 41
mind of the three kayas 6, 43
mirror-like wisdom 3, 35
most fruitional view xviii
mother dakinis 7, 45
mother Prajnaparamita . xvii, 12, 65
Mt. Meru .. 6, 35, 44, 49, 50, 80, 81, 88, 110
Mt. Meru-based world system 50
multicoloured distribution ... 8, 11, 51, 52, 61, 89, 90
murdering butcher 79
musical annotation 70
Nalanda Translation Committee .... xxvi, 113, 114
Nature Great Completion . xviii, xix, 1, 20, 21
nature of mind 86
negativity .... xi, 23
neighing of a horse 14
new translation xx
nine dances 77
nine types of sentient being ... 55
ninefold wishes 9
nine-pointed vajra 2, 30
nine-pointed vajra of meteoric iron 2, 30
nirvana ... v, 3, 8, 13, 33, 54, 55, 67, 75, 76, 78, 80, 81, 96, 113
non-referential meditation ... 40

non-referential meditation on emptiness 40
not stopped 105, 111
Nyang Caves viii
Flower Cave of Great Secrecy . . . . ix, xi
lower cave . . . . ix, xi
upper cave . . . . viii, xi
Nyang Tingdzin Zangpo . viii, xi
Nyingthig . . . . i, iii, v, vii, viii, x, xiii-xx, xxii, 1, 15, 16, 18, 19, 41, 47, 64, 78, 85, 86, 89, 90, 93, 119
Nyingthig Chod . xv, xvii, xx, 18, 19
Nyingthig practitioner . . . xvi, 19
object of refuge 41
object to be cut xix
obscurations . . . . xi, 8, 9, 52, 56
offering that is specific to Chod practice 40
outflows 7, 45, 106
output . . 28, 46, 82, 83, 104, 106
Pacifier Chod . . . . xiv-xx, 86
padma dakini 5, 39
Padma Karpo Translation Committee . . . . i, ii, xxvii, 54, 113, 114
Padmasambhava 7, 20, 45, 46, 102
Pakistan v
paramita . . xv, xvii, 12, 65, 66, 68, 71, 72, 76, 77, 81, 84, 87, 90, 94
paramita of generosity 68
paranormal events 84, 89
Patrul . . i, iii, viii, xiv, xxii, 17, 71, 88, 93, 115
peaceful ones 78
peacock xviii
Phadampa Sangyay xiv
phaṭ 3-10, 12, 13, 33, 35-37, 39, 41, 43, 45, 48, 49, 53, 55-58, 60, 66, 67, 71, 73, 76, 80, 88
phurpa 39
place demons 81
place dons 81
poisonous shrub of samsara xviii
portion
impure 49
pure 49
practice text . . . . xxiii, xxiv
prajna . . . . xv, xvii, 12, 20, 65, 66, 71, 72, 76, 77, 84, 87, 90, 94, 106
Prajnaparamita . . xv, xvii, 12, 65, 66, 72, 76, 84, 87, 90, 94
direct experience of xv
mother xvii
ultimate xv
prayers of aspiration 90, 92
prayers of dedication and aspiration 12, 66
preliminaries . . 40, 72, 84, 87, 91
preserve 84, 90, 107
primordial protector . . . 9, 56, 57
primordial utterance of dharmakaya 36
proud thoughts 80
provocation . . . 12, 23, 62, 65, 92
provocation and finishing 65
provoke and finish 65
pure portion 7, 49
purified, increased, and transformed 8, 50
Purvavideha 3, 35, 80
qualities dakinis 78
queen of the expanse 1, 20
rainbow body 13, 67
rainbow rays 7, 45
Rakshashi 4, 37, 80
rational mind 12, 64, 97, 107
ratna dakini 5, 39

rdzogs pa . . . . v, 15, 102
rdzogs pa chen po 15, 102
recipients of generosity 8, 53
recipients of offering 8, 53
red distribution . 8, 11, 52, 61, 89
referencing 40, 83, 101, 107
requisite articles 1, 22
retribution . 8, 10, 13, 53, 54, 58, 59, 66
retributions . . . 10, 11, 58, 61, 90
revealed treasure . . . xxvi, 18, 60, 70, 119
revealed treasure mark 119
right attitude 27
rigpa . . . ix, 2, 6, 7, 11, 12, 29, 30, 32, 38, 40, 43, 49, 62-64, 79-83, 86, 108, 109, 115
rigpa wisdom ix
roar of a tigress 14
root guru 6, 9, 41, 56, 84
root of self-grasping 6, 45
rousing the right attitude 27
Samantabhadra 57
Samantabhadri 12, 65
Samaya-breaker 4, 36, 37, 81
samsara . . v, xviii, 3, 8, 10, 13, 24, 33, 34, 43, 54, 55, 57, 58, 67, 75, 76, 78, 80, 81, 83, 96, 97, 105, 110
samsara and nirvana 3, 8, 13, 33, 54, 55, 67, 75, 76, 80, 96
samsara and nirvana inseparable 80
samsaric mind . . . xiv, 44, 83, 97, 105, 107, 112
Samye Chimpu viii
sandhi . . . . v, 102
Sanskrit terminology . . . xxvi, 102
second-order thousandfold . . 111
secret wisdom dakini 3, 33
self-arising rigpa 6, 43
self-cherishing . 9, 10, 12, 45, 54, 59, 64, 87
self-cherishing for body . . 10, 59
self-grasping . 3, 5, 6, 33, 36, 38-41, 45, 82
sending and taking 13, 68, 90
sentient being xi, 54, 55, 103, 105
separation of awareness and matter 86
Seven Treasuries . . . . x, xiii
Shechen . . . . xx, xxi, 30, 56, 115, 121, 124-127
Shechen Monastery . . . xx, xxi, 56
sign lineage of the vidyadharas 41
single sphere . . . . xviii, xix, 1, 20
single unique sphere of reality 21, 22
six paramitas 81
sixth buddha 41
skin of a carnivorous beast . 1, 22
skull cup 7, 49, 50
skull drum 4, 9, 37, 54, 55
slaughterhouse 8, 52
small tent1, 3, 5, 22, 24, 32, 38, 83
Sound of Dakini Laughter . . . iii, xiv, xxii, 1, 15, 17, 19, 72, 93
space of dharmakaya 45
space of realization vi, xvii, xix, 33
space-like experience of emptiness 20
special objects of compassion . 59
speech dakinis 78
spirits . . . . xiv, 13, 26, 27, 53, 68, 69, 89
stake 5, 38, 39
stake of enlightenment mind 5, 39
stake of great compassion . . 5, 39
stake of great equanimity . . 5, 39
stake of great joy 5, 39

stake of great loving kindness . 5, 39
stakes of meteoric iron 5, 38
state .. v-vii, ix, xiii, 7, 10, 11, 13, 16, 27, 38, 40, 43, 45, 46, 48, 51, 55, 57, 59, 63, 66, 67, 83, 87, 90, 92, 96-98, 102, 107, 109, 111
state of completion vii
great version vii
lesser vii
state of emptiness ... 10, 11, 59, 63
subjugating visualization .. 2, 28, 73, 74
subjugating visualizations ... 24, 29, 84
subjugation ... 23, 24, 28-30, 73, 74, 84, 94
sub-continents 6, 44
sugatagarbha 47
sun and moon 6, 45, 86
superfactual . xvii, 13, 44, 66, 67, 96, 100, 101, 110
superfactual dharma 13, 67
superfactual truth 100, 101, 110
supports for study ...... iii, 113
sustenance-providing cook ... 79
Swat region of Pakistan v
system of instruction vi
taking refuge 40, 43, 45, 84, 108
temporary experience ... 11, 61, 65, 110
temporary experiences .. 12, 65, 110
terrifying place . 2, 30, 31, 73, 74
the nature ... xix, 21, 83, 86, 88, 89, 103, 104
The Root Volumes of Longchen Nyingthig .... xiii, 119
theism vii
theistic habits vi
thighbone trumpet . 1, 3, 13, 22, 25, 33, 56, 70, 76, 125
thighbone trumpet melodies . 13
thighbone trumpets xvii
third order world 8, 54
third-order thousandfold . 8, 49, 50, 52, 55, 88, 110, 111
Thorough Cut .. xvi, xix, 98, 108
thousandfold realm 7, 49
thousandfold world . 8, 9, 11, 49, 50, 52, 55, 58, 63, 88, 110, 111
three becomings 74, 75
three distributions 51
three doors 87
Three Jewels 43, 91, 108
three kayas .... x, 6, 43, 75
three lineages ... 9, 41, 56, 57, 85
three main subjugations 24
three poisons 74, 106
three realms 55, 69, 74, 75
three roots 8, 41, 43, 53, 89
three secrets 87, 111
three sets of subjugation .. 73, 84
three subjugations 24
three types of generosity 68
Thregcho xvi
Tibetan punctuation xxvi
title of the text 15, 19
transformation of your outlook 11, 61
translation
literal v
Trisong Deutsen xi
troublesome gods and demons 23
true and complete buddhahood vi
Tulku Urgyen ix

two accumulations 9, 11, 45, 56, 61, 77
two obscurations 9, 56
types of retribution 54
Uddiyana v
ultimate enlightenment mind . 44
ultimate Prajnaparamita .. xv, 84
unchanging luminosity ix
uncontrived 6, 13, 43, 67, 92, 111
unification 57, 78
un-outflowed 8, 12, 54, 66, 106, 111
un-outflowed dharmadhatu 12, 66
un-outflowed wisdom 8, 54
upheavals . xiv, 23, 25-27, 62, 64, 65, 84
Upper Cave of Nyang .... viii, xi
Uttarakuru 4, 37, 81
vajra dakini 5, 39
vajra dance 75, 78
vajra essence 7, 46, 47
Vajra Sharpness 71
Vajra Vehicle .. xv, 18, 31, 40, 53, 64, 74, 99-101, 103, 111
Vajra Vehicle feast 53
Vajra Vehicle preliminaries ... 40
Vajradhara 6, 41, 84, 87
Vajrayogini 18, 74
verse for taking refuge 43
vidyadhara gurus 3, 9, 34, 56
view ... xiii, xv, xvi, xviii, xx, 1-3, 11-13, 22, 24, 30, 33, 38, 61, 62, 64, 67, 68, 72, 74, 79, 82, 83, 87, 90, 94, 105
violence of the demons and dons 12, 64
virtuous 12, 66
visualization .... xxii, xxiii, 2, 11, 13, 28, 30, 33, 42, 50, 61, 62, 68, 73, 74, 86-89
visualization of the white skeleton 11, 62
visualization procedures xxii, xxiii
voices of gandharvas 14
wealth of gods and men 6, 45
white distribution 11, 61, 89
white skeleton 11, 62, 63
wisdom .. vii-ix, xii, xiii, xvii, 3-5, 8, 17-19, 33, 35-37, 39, 40, 45-47, 51, 54, 55, 61, 66, 72, 74, 77, 79-81, 97, 98, 105-107, 109-112
wisdom dakini . 3, 33, 36, 40, 47, 61, 74
wisdom dakinis .. xvii, 17-19, 39, 46, 79
wisdom of dharmadhatu 81
wisdom of equality 4, 37, 80
wisdom's self-output 82, 83
wrathful ones 78
Wrathful Woman .. 7, 8, 11, 49, 52, 63, 88, 89
yidam 3, 6, 34, 41, 85
yogic activity . xviii, xx, 1-3, 6, 7, 9, 11, 13, 20-25, 29, 30, 32-35, 43-46, 53, 57, 61, 67, 80
yogic conduct .... xiv-xvii, 22
yogic discipline . xvi, xviii, xxv, 3, 86
yogic lifestyle xvi
yogin .... x, 3, 8, 33, 54, 65

www.ingramcontent.com/pod-product-compliance
Lightning Source LLC
Chambersburg PA
CBHW020052200426
43197CB00049B/372
* 9 7 8 9 9 3 7 8 2 4 4 7 7 *